RISE
RICH

An imprint of The Wealth Building Lab, LLC (Maryland)

© 2025 LaChelle P. Johnson.

Editor
Michelle Schacht

Cover Design
Danna Mathias Steele

Interior Design
Silke Spingies

ISBN Paperback: 979-8-9992822-2-4
ISBN eBook: 979-8-9992822-0-0

Published by Rise Rich Publishing™.

For media inquiries or speaking requests, contact
RiseRich@WealthBuildingLab.org

RISE
INTENTIONAL LIVING FOR FIRST GENERATION WEALTH BUILDERS
RICH

WITH REAL STORIES, MONEY LESSONS,
AND JOURNAL PROMPTS

LACHELLE P. JOHNSON

Dedication

To my grandmothers, Clytie Louise Shanklin-Matthews and Mary Ann Mitchell, smiling down from heaven, whose strength and faith shaped my world in ways words can barely capture. You both survived trying times with unwavering faith, overcame countless challenges, and triumphed over every trial life threw your way. Together, you were the bedrock on which so much of our family's foundation was built. Your sacrifices were immeasurable, and you constantly put your dreams on the back burner so others could move forward. The love and support from you both were a constant, selfless reminder of what it means to truly serve and uplift others.

Grandma Clytie, you always said you wanted to write a book. You urged me to "write everything down," and now, through this book, I'm motivated to take action and relinquish the knowledge and experience God has blessed me to obtain, understand, and communicate in a way that resonates and relates. Losing you left a hole in my heart, but it also ignited a fire in my soul. I now realize how much of my stability and faith were anchored in your existence, and dependent on your consistent prayer over my life, built as strong wings enabling me to fly. Your legacy of triumph, determination, and fullness in life will continue to live on through this manifestation of street and biblical wisdom that will help change the lives of many.

Grandma Mary, you once said to me, "It seems like everything you touch turns to gold." In that light, I pray this book touches many hands, and the words within generate a harvest of life-changing impact that will break generational curses around the world. May it carry forward the spirit of success you saw in me, and plant seeds of mind shifts and faith.

Thank you both for believing in me, for your dreams, and for your eternal influence on my life. May this book bring honor to the powerful women you were on earth and enrich many.

To my parents, I thank you for your love and support. This book throws no shade on all you've done and the efforts you've made. You've loved hard and continue to do the best you can. I love you both infinitely. I'm strong and determined because of you.

With all my love and deepest gratitude,
Tootie

Contents

Dedication   4

Introduction: Your Rich Life, Your Way   8

01   Starting From the Same Place   10

02   Ditch the Scarcity Mindset   13

03   Align Your Money with Your Vision   24

04   Rise with Purpose   35

05   Maximizing Credit & Scores   49

06   Wise Saving   65

07   Break Free   75

08   Rise Within, Then Extend   84

09   Rich Is More than Money   99

10   Intentional Investing   104

11   Understanding Income Taxes – A Foundation for Beginners   121

12   The Power of Generosity and Giving Back   132

13   Your Legacy Starts with You   144

Daily Affirmations for the Journey Ahead   156

A Concluding Message from the Author   158

Introduction:
Your Rich Life, Your Way

For too long, money has been treated like the end goal, something people want more and more of without a sense of what they really need it all for. It's been something to chase, something to compare, something that measures whether we've "made it" or not. But here's the truth: money isn't the goal; money is a tool. The real goal is building your rich life, a life that reflects your values, your vision, and your unique path, and the reality is you may not need as much as you're chasing after all.

This book isn't about copying someone else's definition of success or realizing what society has defined as the "American Dream". It's about uncovering your own rich life vision. Comparison is a trap that robs us of joy and clarity. When you spend your life measuring yourself against someone else's highlight reel, you lose sight of the fact that your journey is personal, your needs are different, and your purpose is yours alone. A rich life is not one-size-fits-all; it's about rising in the areas that matter most to you.

For some, being rich might mean owning a home, investing early, and leaving wealth for future generations. For others, it might look like traveling the world, giving back to their community, or having the freedom to spend time with family without worrying about bills. Being rich is more than dollars in the bank, it is focus on how you spend your time, how you enjoy your life, and how you design your days with intention.

Throughout this book, we'll shift our focus from just surviving to truly living. You'll learn how to use money with purpose, not as something that controls you, but as a resource to build the life you envision. You'll reflect, plan, and take action, not only to grow your finances, but to grow your peace, your joy, and your impact.

This is your guided journey to break cycles, build wealth, and rise into the life you were created to live. So, let go of comparison. This is about your rise. Your money, your time, your lifestyle, your rich life – shaped with intention and lived on purpose.

Don't immerse yourself in this book as if it's just words on paper, it's a guide, a journal, and a roadmap for your journey. As you move through each chapter, you'll find principles, practical steps, wisdom, exercises, and journal prompts designed to help you act and see real change in your life. Don't just read. Engage. Write. Reflect. Apply. Every exercise is a chance to put what you've learned into motion.

Your rich life is waiting, and each page is a step closer. So, let's begin. Let's shift your mindset, strengthen your money habits, and build the foundation for a future filled with freedom, purpose, and joy. Your rise is personal, and it starts now.

01 Starting From the Same Place

Before we dive in, I want to set the stage for this book, so we all start with the same understanding. Each chapter is designed to take you closer to the vision you have for being rich, while sharing both street and biblical wisdom. The information and experiences I share are taken directly from my personal life. I am living proof that a Rich life is possible.

Let's start by breaking down the various perspectives we'll use and make clear what "Hood" and "Rich" mean for the purpose of this book.

The look of your Hood may be slightly different given your geographic area, but at their core, most Hoods have the same characteristics:

Hood – a culturally rich but often economically challenged neighborhood that fosters resilience, identity, and survival among its residents who are also facing violence, drugs, poverty, external judgement, and systemic neglect.

Rich (from Hood to Rich) – living in overflow, not just with money, but also with freedom, purpose, and peace. It's breaking cycles, building wealth, and creating a life you weren't born into but were born for.

Being Rich in this context means:

- Having options, not just income
- Making choices from vision, not survival
- Growing money and multiplying
- Leaving more than you inherited
- Owning your time, your mindset, and your future

You're rich when you stop living check to check and start living choice to choice.

The rise to rich is personal, and it encompasses everything that makes you feel the ultimate level of peace, freedom, and fulfillment.

What Could Rich Look Like for You?

In terms of finances, Rich means having an abundance of money, assets, or wealth. You could be someone with a high income, large savings, varied investments, and financial freedom.

However, being Rich can also mean having what you need on a personal level, such as peace, health, time, love, and purpose. For example, imagine yourself as a person who lives debt-free, travels, gives freely, and enjoys meaningful relationships. You might consider yourself rich as such, even without millions.

In many communities and cultures, especially those over-coming hardship, Rich might mean:

- Breaking generational cycles
- Creating options
- Being able to help others
- Living with dignity and self-determination
- Keeping family traditions alive from generation to generation

And do not forget there is a biblical or spiritual definition of Rich. True richness may be defined as abundance in faith, wisdom, favor, and eternal purpose, not solely material wealth. The Bible yields many examples of blessings and richness, and states variations of the word more than 100 times. God calls us to live a life that is exceedingly abundant beyond what we could ever imagine. As such, "The blessing of the Lord makes rich, and He adds no sorrow with it" (Prov. 10:22).

What's important is the intention you put behind defining Rich for your life. The sooner you do this, the less time and money you will waste on things that really don't matter.

02 Ditch the Scarcity Mindset

Your mindset is what drives the decisions you make with your money. The workings of the human mind are the result of intricate brain functions combined with experiences, emotions, and external influences. Our mind not only processes information, but it's the command center for how we think, feel, and act.

Growing up in survival mode in the Hood, your first education about money comes from the streets, whether that's your neighborhood, your household, or your hustle. You learn fast: money comes and goes. Sometimes it's feast, most times it's famine. That kind of experience wires your mind a certain way to survive, not to build.

My Story

I am a product of a teen pregnancy, who grew up in the trenches of Landover, Maryland, a city in Prince George's County, where money was something borrowed more than had. It was insufficient, a stressor, a mystery, and/or something we assumed people who lived in single-family homes had plenty of. Conversations about building good credit or wealth never happened around the family dinner table, or anywhere else for that matter. The primary and consistent concern was stretching meals to ensure food lasted for the week and mastering the use of shoe polish to help keep the annual pair fresh K-Swiss looking fresh. These, Reebok Classics, or Princess Reeboks were the tennis shoe staple for the teenage girls in the early nineties.

In the Hood, the way in which dollars were assigned to essential needs required monthly, even weekly, prioritization because there wasn't enough money to fully cover expenses in most households. It wasn't uncommon for parents to lean on their kids' virgin credit to bounce back from a delinquent account to keep the lights on or the water running. Living paycheck to paycheck was more of an art than a science.

Dollars were thinly spread and creatively made. Entrepreneurship was actually pretty common, although in some cases illegal. There were candy ladies, stationed ice cream trucks, drug dealers, hair stylists, palm readers, mechanics – you name it, we had it. The community relied heavily on the products and services conveniently situated and easy to access. Get rich quick schemes and fast money antics played in the midst of beggars and addicts trying to borrow from whomever they could. I remember getting my palm read by an illegitimate psychic, and suffering from nightmares afterwards for a week. I didn't know any better and, to make matters worse, I actually paid her for it.

The Hood provided zero education or exposure to the concept of building wealth. Only dreams of being Hood Rich, and the reality of that seemed far-fetched. Hood Rich life goals were immediate, personal, and pleasurable. Soap operas and juke boxes were considered necessities! After making enough money to pay bills, it was all partying, buying the latest fashion fads and trends, and indulging in the "be seen" social scene. Hood Rich life required endless amounts of cash to splurge on these things until the money ran out.

Eager to gain financial stability and independence, I started looking for work before I was even legally able to. I had my mind on my money, and my money on my mind. I landed my first job at the age of fourteen with All City Sportswear, a T-shirt stand in the middle of what used to be the Landover Mall. With that paycheck, the money started rolling in every two weeks. I didn't have any responsibilities or bills, nor did I even think about saving. Living Hood Rich was now within reach...well, the image I wanted to portray was anyway. I wanted to buy all the things I couldn't get my hands on when I was broke. I am a true witness that "past-perceived voids create present-pursued values" as Dr. Myron Golden said.[1] In other words, the material things I couldn't afford before had even more worth to me now that I had the means to buy them, whether they had that value or not. With a regular cashflow, if you were looking for me, you probably could find me shopping for clothes, shoes, or beauty supplies. Two years later, a car, cell phone, and tattoos consumed my thoughts. My mindset was to simply spend the money I had on all the things I wanted or needed to do.

Then, the debt started piling. After receiving my driver's license at age sixteen, I tapped into our neighborhood car salesman. He went to car auctions every month, bought old cars, minimally repaired them so they would last at least a year, then resell them. I purchased my first car from him for a whopping $400! It was a gold, Plymouth Reliant I named "Goldie" that barely got me from point A to B. I didn't realize the effort involved in trying to keep that car running safely. It was an expensive chore that cost me a lot of time and money. After the transmission blew, I figured it was time I graduate to paying a car note, which came with the responsibility of carrying expensive car insurance.

----

1   Dr. Myron Golden is a well-known Christian entrepreneur, business growth consultant, motivational speaker, and author who teaches biblical principles for business and personal development. He keeps an active YouTube channel: https://www.youtube.com/@MyronGolden/featured

It turned into what seemed like a cycle every couple years... though unconscious to me. The more I made, the more I told myself I could afford, spending up every dime. But, because I was paying my accumulating bills so smartly (I thought), I did not perceive any problems. The offers to save 20 percent for opening new credit card accounts were irresistible no-brainers since I thought, if I use the credit card, that'll keep more cash in my pocket to hold me over until next pay day. And I didn't hesitate to use these cards because I knew my minimum payment on each account was only about $30 a month— I could afford that! I was living a life I felt was above the average adult in my neighborhood. Life was good. I could help my mom buy things, and I could buy good gifts for Christmas. I could buy what I wanted, when I wanted it, and if not right then, it was on the list for my next paycheck. My money was often spent on a list of things I had in mind before I even got paid. You can see how I dove into debt headfirst.

Though I lived paycheck to paycheck, I understood credit card balances needed to be paid. With debt came a strong sense of responsibility, especially as my debt pile grew bigger and heavier every year. I started to feel the burden of the debt trap I had led myself into. I made sure to hit the minimum payment requirements on time, but I continuously looked for ways to earn more money to keep up. But I must say there was something about getting mail in my name from a credit card company that made me feel like I had it going on. I just knew I was BALLINNN! I felt like the debt I was accruing only elevated my economic status, so I had to make sure I kept my credit intact, so they'd approve my requests for increases. I treated credit increases like a pay raise. How crazy was that thinking!

I had officially entered my own world of trying to alleviate feeling the struggle and become financially stable and secure in the most roundabout Hood-way of justified thinking. It was a stressful situation, but it forced me to lean into my faith and focus on ways to raise my income and ultimately become the most successful version of myself.

I found myself seeking out opportunities for scholarships and attending seminars that could potentially set me on a pathway to college. I hadn't taken the ACT or SAT, and my parents were unfamiliar with the process. My mom went straight to work after completing her general education degree (GED), and my dad went into the Airforce shortly after graduating high school. In time, I landed at Prince George's Community College of Largo, Maryland, pursuing an associate's degree in business and management. I received enough grant funding through both state- and federally funded tuition assistance programs to cover my tuition and was a recipient of the Apartment and Office Building Association (AOBA) scholarship. This was a great start with more than enough money to cover all costs, but coming from a household where money was scarce, and being relatively financially illiterate, the additional student loan offers from the U.S. Department of Education were an attractive add to my refund status.

Now a full-time college student, I didn't realize I was moving from debt traps to debt prison after accepting the full extent of student loan offers. I took full advantage of them without ever considering or questioning why they consistently offered me more than what I needed to cover my tuition, housing, and books. Nope, I just looked forward to cashing out on all my refunds at the end of each semester as if they were lottery hits. My student loan debt was racking up alongside my credit card debt. My mind kept telling me repayments were sooooooo far away that I didn't need to worry about student loan bills. Like, who's thinking about life in twenty to thirty years at my young age? By that time, I figured, I would have a better job and be able to pay my loans with no problem. I was just happy I could finally say goodbye to the days of shopping for one pair of tennis shoes to last the entire school year with more than a fair share of shoe polish, and hello to blowing every dollar I had on whatever I wanted. This mindset was immature and ignorant, causing me to dig debt holes so big that most lower and maybe even some middle-class folks would feel like it's impossible to climb out of.

Here's What I Learned

The unbelievable reality is that you can have a good job and still be broke. You can win the lottery and still go bankrupt. You can win in a get-rich-quick scheme today, and the money can be gone tomorrow. Why?

> If your mind isn't ready to manage money,
> it won't matter how many ways
> you figure out how to make it.

No matter how hard you work to bring in money, it'll continue to flow out just as fast, if not faster, if you don't value your relationship with it, and manage it accordingly.

Street Truth: If you don't control your mind, society will.

People who don't respect money end up broke, even when they get tons of money. I know people who flipped $500 into $5,000 with a hustle, and others who blew a $150,000 settlement like it was play money. I also know entrepreneurs who have a cash flow of more than $20,000 per month and hit a $0 balance before the next month starts. The difference isn't the source or amount of money. It is their mindset.

You can have street smarts and still be broke if your mindset hasn't shifted from surviving to thriving. It's important to value every dollar and consciously focus on directing it to places that put you in a better position.

Biblical Wisdom: Becoming rich and generating wealth doesn't start with a number. It starts with a new way of thinking.

Romans 12:2 says, *"Be transformed by the renewing of your mind."*

Notice this verse does not say your paycheck. Or your job title. Instead, it says your mind. Renewing your mind, or in other words, shifting its perspective, is what allows you to transform your relationship with money.

Rise Rich Exercise:
Three Ways to Shift Your Mindset

You cannot reach a goal if you cannot first visualize it. With your dream rich lifestyle in mind, I want you to commit yourself to going from ... (your starting point) to ... (your finishing line) with each statement below. Let's reprogram your way of thinking in this way.

01 Scarcity to Abundance

A scarcity view is based on fear. A view from eyes that see abundance is one that brings peace.

- Scarcity says, "There's not enough, I gotta get mine before someone else does."
- Abundance says, "There's more than enough for everyone, including me."

Repeat to yourself: *Everything I have is a resource I'm responsible for, even if it's small.* Start with the assets, knowledge, money, and resources you have accessible to you now **and use them wisely.** In other words, don't waste your seed and expect a harvest. Your seeds come in the form of time, money, and information. Think about all the ways you can capitalize or monetize what you have in these respects and then be sure your efforts are planted in such a way that they return a fruitful harvest. Jesus said, *"Whoever is faithful with little will be faithful with much"* (Luke 16:10).

02 Quick Money to Smart Money

On the street, the truth is: *Fast money comes with fast problems.*

Dating drug dealers, shopping with thieves, and spending time trying to get rich quick results in a lot of time and money lost. Not to mention it brings trouble that takes you way off track in ways that can take years to recover mentally, financially, and spiritually. The risk isn't worth the time or the perceived to be rewards. From my experience, taking risks associated with any of them only keeps you in a revolving cycle of spending, hustling, and earning, just to do it all over again with zero realized gain or profit.

Real wealth building takes wisdom, patience, and self-control. That means not getting caught up in get-rich-quick schemes or impressing people who aren't paying your bills.

Proverbs 13:11 says, "Wealth gained hastily will dwindle, but whoever gathers little by little will increase it."

03 From Consumer to Creator

Growing up in the Hood, there isn't much training around saving, so most of us, by default, focus on spending. Real power comes when you shift to ownership—of your time, your money, your mindset, your skills.

You don't need a million to think like a millionaire.

You might be thinking, *"That sounds great, but it is too far-fetched. I'm just trying to pay bills."*

Instead of fighting or doubting this mindset, start asking yourself, *"How can I expand my knowledge and multiply my money, starting with what I have, and growing from here?"*

 **Journal Entry #1**
Write & Reflect: I Am Fully Capable of Renewing my Mind

01 How do I view my current relationship with money?

....
....
....

02 Do I relate to any of these money lessons? Which ones do I have in common that are unhealthy or limiting for me?

....
....
....

03 What does it mean for me to be a good steward over what I have right now?

....
....
....

04 If God gave me more today, would I be ready to handle it or would I waste it?

....
....
....

Take One Step Closer to Your Richer Life

You don't need to have a lot to begin your wealth-building efforts. You just need to begin with what you've got. Living a Rise Rich life starts here, in your mind, in your heart, in your daily choices.

Block out the distractions of that social media lifestyle-hype or trying to keep up with the Jones's. Replace this time spent scrolling or dwelling on what you don't have, comparing yourself to others, with being laser focused on the larger vision you have for your life. Understand, believe, and trust this process. You'll begin to see a subtle shift that will grow stronger in how you value time and money. You will start treating every minute of your life, and dollar in your pocket, like a valued treasure that cannot be wasted, and you will choose to use both with intentional purpose not just for the moment, but for your future.

03 Align Your Money with Your Vision

You can't build anything—whether it's a tower, a business, or a better life, if you don't know what you've got to work with from the start. The same concept applies to wealth building. You must determine what tools, skills, resources, and knowledge you have. But a lot of us were never taught how to track money. We were taught to hustle until payday, pay what we could, and pray we had enough gas money till Friday. That's not a wealth plan. That's a cycle.

Money cycles don't break on accident; they break when you face your finances head-on. Even if the numbers hurt. Even if you've been avoiding them. You must know where you are to get where you're going.

"Suppose one of you wants to build a tower. Won't you first sit down and estimate the cost…?"(Luke 14:28 NIV).

My Story

I was running out of money every month fast. Even though I kept an accurate check book ledger (back then before convenient baking apps existed, we did it all in writing), cash flow was difficult because I'd find myself hitting negative zero quite often.

What came in was a fixed amount, but I was steadily increasing what needed to be paid out. This placed me in a vicious cycle of trying to bring in more money to pay out more money. The crush became so tight I had to search for ways to reduce my expenses as well as find ways to make more money. I fell for just about any side hustle that came my way. Spending lump sums of money on multilevel marketing start up fees (Mary Kay, Body Magic, It Works—you name it, I tried it!), stocking inventory to meet potential on demand sales and accepting auto shipments for my own supply, which were typically more than I needed. I was successful just as long as momentum for the trend and clientele was high. I made a few dollars but didn't track the money to see if I made a profit on my initial investment. I treated my side hustles like get rich quick schemes, and, before I knew it, I was burned out and looking for the next opportunity high. That cycle became a revolving door in my young adult years, making it very easy to rake in more and more debt as money continued to fly right on out the window!

I learned very quickly that impulse decisions are a trick of the enemy…Satan that is. Life is all about choices, decisions, and consequences, which have positive or negative effects. The devil comes to steal, kill, and destroy, so he is the advocate for failure. When I fully realized this, I made a point to give myself twenty-four hours to think rationally and digest the facts before deciding whether or not the thing I was considering aligned with the vision and goals I had set for myself. I learned to say NO to impulse spending. Not only is it important to be in alignment with the plan God has for your life, but it's also even more important to know that the devil is waiting in the wings, instilling fear and self-doubt, advocating for us to fail.

Here's What I Learned

Respect every dollar and do not focus on lack or what you wish you had. Sometimes it's difficult when eighty percent of the time you were witness to the struggle of keeping food on the table, the lights on, and the water running. It wasn't hard for my mind to flashback to the times I had to sit at the kitchen table for hours and force food down despite being full because I was taught wasting was forbidden. In a state of scarcity, we were constantly reminded by our superiors that there were people starving around the world and food cost money, so we dare not waste it. It is important to appreciate what you have, but, by the same token, we must be able to visualize how close abundance is in reach. The constant focus on scarcity often keeps our vision close to that state.

Street Truth: In the streets, nobody walks into a game of craps without knowing what's in their pocket.

If you've got $20 to your name, you make $20 decisions. Why? Because slipping up could cost you everything... including your life. Trust me, I know multiple people shot dead for not being able to pay gambling debts. Money is a serious matter as it impacts livelihoods from all extremes. Nas got it right in the 1999 Nastradamus album with his song, "Money Makes the World Go Round."

It's easy to become very relaxed when it comes to our bank accounts. It's easy to stop tracking the true balance. We guess. We swipe those credit cards and hope. I've been there, and it didn't feel good when the waiter brought my bank card back to the table because its funds weren't sufficient to pay my bill.

Biblical Wisdom: Vision Is a Spiritual Principle

God is a visionary. Every promise in Scripture started with a plan. God blessed those who followed His word with land, purpose, direction, and more.

Habakkuk 2:2 says, *"Write the vision and make it plain, so that he who reads it may run with it."*

Your financial vision should be so clear, it gives you the motivation to run—not just stroll—toward the life you want. Your plan should excite you to shift your mind from being emotionally reactive to external influences that will constantly wipe out your bank account to focusing on a purposeful, strategic financial vision filled with stable money goals.

Rise Rich Exercise: *Your Rich Life Vision*

Before we get to money, I want you to map out a clear vision for your life. Proceed with a clear mind and take a break if needed to do so. This planning step is critical, and clarity is important. It will help keep you focused on the action steps directed in this book. Follow these simple steps to document your Rich Life Vision. Write your answers in detail.

01 Reflect on Your Core Values
Ask yourself:

- What truly matters to me?
- What do I stand for?
- What kind of legacy do I want to leave?

Tip: Choose 3–5 core values. Examples include freedom, faith, family, service, growth, etc.

02 Picture Your Rich Life
Visualize your future and ask:

- Where do I live?
- What kind of work do I do?
- How do I spend my time?
- Who is around me?

03 Define Success on Your Terms
This is not society's version of success; it's yours. In your dictionary, success could mean peace of mind, financial independence, strong relationships, spiritual growth, or something else entirely.

04 Break Your Vision into Life Domains
Clarify your vision for each area. Details are important.

- Spiritual
- Family & Relationships
- Career/Business
- Health
- Finances
- Personal Growth

05 Write a Personal Vision Statement
Summarize your dream Rich Life in a powerful sentence or two. This will be your mantra, the reminder of your vision and goals.

Here's mine:

"I am a financially free woman who honors God, leads my family with love, and serves my community with purpose. I live a life of peace, joy, and impact."

About ten years ago, I set out to be financially free enough to travel when and where I wanted, to get my three children through college without the need for loans, and to retire by the age of fifty-five with the stability to maintain my rich lifestyle. I also decided I would peacefully and intentionally dictate the direction of my time and money to build generational wealth.

I'm grateful to report, as I write this book, I am debt free with an 800 plus credit score, with my first kid approaching his senior in college student loan free. I travel when and where I want, and I am in the process of gaining more ownership of my time as I approach retirement (on track to do so before age fifty-five). I am living proof these money concepts work, and I am beyond happy to provide you with a shortcut.

Everything you do, and every dollar you make, should align with the process needed to achieve the goals that will turn your vision into reality.

 ## *Rise Rich Exercise:*
Where Is Your Money Going?

Getting back to the money, there is no way you can be intentional about building wealth if you have no control over where your money is going. You've got to take ownership, and when I say own it, I mean be the dictator of your money. You're going to tell it where to go instead of impassively seeing where it goes, and you're going to actively assign your dollars to align with your vision.

01 Track Your Income

Let's get real: You can't grow what you don't track. You have no control if you aren't tracking the dollars and cents. You don't have to be rich to budget, and just because you budget doesn't mean you can't live a fulfilling life. You only have to be serious and disciplined to build the lifestyle you want.

Start with writing it down. Every income stream, from every place you have money coming in.

- Paychecks
- Side hustles
- Child support
- Government assistance
- Business gigs, tips, etc.

HUGE MISTAKE: Most people stop here and go on about their business. This is what I did for years. I thought if I made more and more money, I'd eventually have more than enough to live out my Rich Life. That way of thinking was FALSE HOPE. As I've said, the more I made, the more I spent, and I couldn't quite recall where all my money went by the end of the month.

You might feel like you're always working, but still broke. You have to face the fact that it's not always an income issue; it's often from leaks in your financial boat. Hustle harder if you need to but hustle smarter by plugging the holes.

For example, you might be spending too much time on gigs that are costing you more than just money. Remember, all money isn't good money. Be very thoughtful about how you spend your time and consider if it's worth the money you're receiving in return. Can your time be focused on something elsewhere in the short term that will bring you greater returns?

02 Write Down Your Bills and Spending

You MUST allocate time for this. Most people shy away from this step and stay stuck because they're scared to face the truth. But the truth sets you free (John 8:32).

Grab your bank statements, pull up your credit card statements, and scroll through your cash apps as you need to. Get a detailed list of what you're spending your money on every month:

- Rent/mortgage
- Food, including groceries, restaurants, fast food, take-out
- Gas or transit expenses, like bus fare or Uber
- Cell phone
- Utilities
- Subscriptions for streaming services, apps, and the like
- Gym memberships, special health gear or food
- Vacations, weekend getaways, other personal travel
- Personal habits, such as smoking, drinks, nails, hair, gambling, lottery, etc.

Now, pause and take some time to add up all your expenses. How are you looking? It is often said that you put your money where your priorities are and easily overspend because there's a clear connection to the perceived value of what you get out of the expense. The more you keep watch on your spending, the more your priorities can be intentionally monitored so you aren't haphazardly going overboard.

It wasn't until I shifted my mindset to truly value every dollar and being intentional about putting my money to work for me that I understood how important it is to track my spending. It certainly helps me keep my impulse spending in check. Now I totally get why Oprah, and many other filthy rich people personally approve individual payments. My results after completing this exercise for the first time was jaw dropping! Let me say, my food, shopping, and entertainment costs were more than my car note every month. Why? I'm a foodie! I rarely spared any expense when it came to a quality, fine dining experience. Concerts and shopping to prepare for vacations, that money was a no brainer because the excitement around the experience made every dime worth it in my mind. Writing down these expenditures uncovered the fact that I needed boundaries and limitations around how much and how often I splurged on these things. It was necessary that they remain part of my desired lifestyle, but within reason, because I realized some of that money could be making money if it was sitting in a high-yield savings account.

03 Create a Simple Lifestyle Tracker

This rewording turns the notion of a "restricted budget" into a realistic "lifestyle expense tracker" that doesn't sacrifice the things that make us feel happy and fulfilled on this financial journey. Now, not everyone will have tons of leftover money... and that's okay. We'll work with what you got to get to where you want.

Managing your money with authority and intention will help you accomplish your financial goals much faster. Take charge and tell your money where to go instead of wondering where it went cluelessly a week after pay day.

Start simple:

01 List your total income
02 Subtract your fixed expenses (rent, car, cell phone, subscriptions, utilities, etc.)

03 Plan for other variable expenses (food, gas, entertainment, birthdays)

This budget doesn't have to be perfect. However, it has to be honest. It's okay if your balance is zero, or even negative zero. Mine fell into the negative month after month for many years. Let's keep going, though. I'll tell you how to fix that.

Journal Entry #2
Write & Reflect: Being Transparent with Myself

01 How do I feel when I look at my bank account? Why?

....

....

....

02 Where do I spend money emotionally? Am I trying to lift my spirits or sense of self in an area of my life? Am I attempting to solve boredom, stress, or impressing others?

....

....

....

03 What's one spending habit you can shift this week that would move you closer to controlling your money?

....

....

....

04 What's one spending habit you can shift this week that is a step toward your rich lifestyle goal?

....

....

....

Take One Step Closer to Your Richer Life

Wealth doesn't start when you "get more money." It starts when you take control of what you already have. Even if it's not much, God can multiply it – if you manage it.

"Whoever can be trusted with very little can also be trusted with much..." (Luke 16:10).

04 Rise with Purpose

Money without purpose is just paper; it comes in and goes out without changing anything. But when you attach your money to clear, personal goals, it becomes fuel for your rise. Goal setting is where vision meets discipline; it's the process of deciding not just what you want, but why you want it, and creating a financial plan that reflects those priorities. Managing money with intention means every dollar has a mission: some to cover your needs, some to attack debt, some to build savings, and some to create opportunities for the future. In this chapter, you'll learn how to set financial goals that actually inspire you, align your spending with your vision, and track progress in a way that keeps you motivated. The goal isn't just to manage money, it's to command it with purpose so it moves you closer to the life you're called to live.

My Story

"The moment she held her child,
  she didn't just become a mother,
  she became a warrior with a purpose"

– author unknown

In my early twenties, not only was I a full-time grad student and mom of a toddler, but I was also a full-time employee. I knew it was critically important to my future to keep juggling all these balls in the air 24/7. I still didn't understand the business of money or how to manage it, so mentally, I was hard wired to just keep working hard to finish my degree. This was the only plan I had: To make more money, I needed to work hard so I could get promoted so I could make more money in order to buy into all the multi-level marketing presentations I went to so I could find ways to make more money. Now, while I do believe hard work pays off, what I wish I knew then was how to slow down and be more strategic with the money I was making and the time I was spending on all these efforts. I spent years walking in faith and waiting for things to fall into place so my money would catch up with my bills and responsibilities. I purchased a home (with zero knowledge of real estate investing), which added to my expenses, then sold it for a larger home (ended up being a bad investment, but it looked like an upgrade) and increased my expenses again (house poor here we come!).

The grind was real, and it was emotionally rewarding being able to live self-sufficiently, but the reality was that the lack of financial education literally made my journey equal to going around and around a monopoly board, paying $200 to pass "GO" with no strategy to win. I was simply grinding to fulfill societal norms under what was believed to be the generally-stated American Dream—to one day move out of my mom's house, buy a house, get married, have two children (a boy and a girl), and live happily ever after. I managed, spent, and invested my money aimlessly without clear strategy. I used it without any direction or financial goals in mind. I was experiencing increase yet still living paycheck to paycheck. It was like being stuck in an Escape Room with no clues to find a way out.

I will say it again, though I admit to feeling like a broken record, *If I only knew then what I know now.* The primary purpose of money is NOT to pay bills or strive to make it so we can pay bills and buy things (we can't really afford). This is how poor people remain poor. Knowledge of how to get out and stay out of the debt trap is power. Learning how to make your money work for you and fund your rich lifestyle without being stressed while living it is powerful. The primary purpose of money IS to put it to work in areas that generate more of it and create valuable returns. Direct your money in ways that pay you dividends, interest income, and invaluable experiences. By doing this, you not only gain financial freedom, but you will also buy some time back by no longer spinning in spending cycles that keep you broke. I started looking at my life based on my end goal, which was the lifestyle I wanted to live when I was financially free enough to do so. That included where I wanted to live, what I wanted to live in, what car I wanted to drive, what memberships and lifestyle amenities I wanted to maintain, how often I wanted to travel, how much I wanted to support my children to kick start their road to independence, how much I wanted to be able to pass down generationally, and more. Everyone's desires might look different in each respect, but when you start with your heart's desires, you can become more intentional and strategic about making the end goal a reality. We'll look more into how it's done as you read along.

Here's What I Learned

Street Truth: If you don't set a target, you can't miss it, but you also hit nothing.

A lot of people avoid goals because they're scared of falling short. But listen, fear of failure is a luxury you can't afford when you're trying to break cycles. Your goals don't have to be fancy. They just have to be real and true to what will help you live a peaceful life with financial freedom — that's what this book defines as rich.

Think of reaching your goals in the same manner as a GPS provides directions as you drive. It reroutes as your course does. You might be forced to take detours because of road blockages. You might hit traffic that slows down your forward progress. But the GPS plan flexes and charts a new course to your final destination and keeps you from quitting halfway through the drive. Can you see the analogy to you, your money, and achieving your financial vision?

01 Sacrifice Builds Discipline

True financial discipline doesn't start with abundance; it starts with the willingness to say no, even to yourself. That means skipping the trendy shoes to build your emergency fund. It means cutting back on eating out, so your credit card balance finally goes down. Sacrifice isn't punishment, it's power. Each time you make a wise decision, you're exercising financial muscles that will serve you for life.

02 Evaluate and Be Tough

Impulse buying, emotional spending, and comparison to others can sabotage your budget. Get in the habit of pausing before every purchase: Ask yourself the hard questions: Do I need this immediately? Is there a reason I want this right now; is it practical or emotional? Do I own something else I can make do with or use instead? Will it bless my future or burden it? Asking these questions and saying "no" to yourself is a habit you can build, and, over time, it leads to freedom, not lack. You'll be proud you learned this skill.

03 Become Obsessed with Paying Lenders

Your lenders shouldn't be the people you're most generous with. Think of them like the character of Scrooge in the story *A Christmas Carol*, who is always trying to find a way to take more of your money. They run their business centered on what's best for them. High-interest debt is like pouring your wealth into someone else's pocket. Make a boss move by paying more than the minimum payment on your credit card or other loans. Treat debt payoff like your side hustle. List your debts in your Lifestyle Tracker and hit them with everything you've got.

> **Biblical Wisdom:** God Honors Order
>
> God is not a God of chaos. He honors order, stewardship, and preparation.
>
> Proverbs 27:23 says, *"Be sure you know the condition of your flocks, give careful attention to your herds."*
> In today's world, your "flocks" are your income, your expenses, your assets, and your time. If you don't know what you've got, how can you manage it wisely?

God doesn't bless mess. However, He will bless your effort when you get intentional.

Rise Rich Exercise:
The Three Money Goal Levels

Let's have you practice goal setting. Highlight the goals you need or would like to tackle at each level below. Feel free to add goals to these sections as you see fit. The Rise is personal on your journey to live Rich.

01 Survival-to-Stability—Short-Term Goals (0–12 months)
- Build $500–$1,000 emergency fund
- Pay off credit cards using the snowball effect *(don't close any...I'll share why later)*
- Save for a move *(if you must)*
- Start budgeting using your Lifestyle Tracker monthly

02 Level Up—Mid-Term Goals (1–5 years)
- Pay off student loans
- Increase income by $10k/year
- Save for a car or home down payment
- Improve credit score to 700+

03 Legacy Building—Long-Term Goals (5–20+ years)
- Own a home or rental property
- Start a business
- Save for college
- Fully fund retirement
- Leave an inheritance (Proverbs 13:22)

Turn Your Dreams into Action: The SMART Goal Formula is a very common business practice used by CEOs of successful businesses. The letters stand for specific, measurable, achievable, relevant, and timebound; and these words serve as the parameters guiding your efforts. They help you set a clear focus around goals you're motivated to be accountable to, fueling better decision making that ensures your financial resources are tracked and spent efficiently toward rich life goal achievements.

Set Rise Rich goals that are SMART, like the examples provided for each category below:

- Specific – Not too vague or broad
    - "Save $6,000 to start my emergency fund," not "Save more"
    - "Pay off $3,000 in credit card debt," not "Pay down one of my credit cards"
    - "Raise my 401(k) contribution from 5% to 7%," not "Save more to plan for retirement"

- Measurable – Trackable with numbers
    - Deposit $500 per month in my savings account
    - Make $300 extra payments monthly in addition to the minimum
    - Increase deductions by 1% every quarter

- Achievable – Realistic based on where you are
    - Adjust budget to cut $125 a week on "wants" that I don't "need"
    - Use a side hustle income stream to cover the payments
    - Offset by cutting $100 a month from non-essential subscriptions

- Relevant – Aligned with your lifestyle vision
  - Builds financial security and reduces reliance on credit cards
  - Reduces interest payments and improves credit scores
  - Grows retirement savings for long-term wealth

- Time-bound – Has a deadline
  - Reach $6,000 in 12 months
  - Eliminate balance in 10 months
  - Reach 7% contribution rate within 3 months

Complete SMART Goal Example: "I will save $500 in 3 months by setting aside $42 a week and cutting my Uber Eats spending. This will help me start my emergency fund and prepare me to overcome financial emergencies as they arise."

Now, this is where most people start to sweat because you have to constantly deny your flesh and own up to bad spending habits. That's uncomfortable. So, to make the process less stressful and keep life feeling fulfilled, let's consider a few more things.

Here's the good news: You can enjoy life *while* you build!

Let's be real: what's the point of building a wealthy, Rise Rich life if you're miserable the whole way there? God didn't call us to struggle endlessly in the name of discipline. He called us to wisdom, contentment, and joy. Ecclesiastes 3:13 says, *"Everyone should eat and drink and take pleasure in all their toil—this is God's gift to man."*

So, yes – save, budget, pay off debt. But also live.

Here's how to enjoy the ride without wrecking your goals:

01 Celebrate Progress, Not Just Perfection

What if you set a SMART savings goal and hit only 70% of it? Celebrate. That's an amazing job!

What if you didn't overspend this week? That's a win worth a pat on the back, too.

Treat small victories like big ones. Each success, no matter its size, means your mindset is shifting. And, when I say each success, that's *everything*.

Street Truth: Motivation runs out. Rewards keep you going.

02 Budget for Joy

Every dollar has a job. And one of those jobs can be pleasure. Even if it's $10 to $20 a month, set aside money for:

- A good meal
- A movie
- Coffee with a friend
- A hobby you love

This isn't wasted money, it's what keeps you from burning out and giving up.

03 Find Ways to Take Breaks that Are Free or Low-Cost

Wealthy people understand this: rest and joy are investments, not luxuries. A person cannot function at their best without taking time to recharge.

Joy doesn't have to be expensive. You can:

- Take walks in new neighborhoods exploring the sights
- Host game nights or potlucks to enjoy the company and laughter of friends
- Volunteer together as a family and give back
- Visit local free events, festivals, museums, etc. to expand your knowledge and have fun
- Spend time in nature and breathe the fresh air

04 Build a Happy Feelings List

Create a list of 10 to 20 things that make you feel alive, refreshed, happy, or inspired. Not things that cost a lot, just things that celebrate your spirit and make you *you*.

Examples include:

- Dancing in the kitchen
- Reading a good book
- Taking your shoes off in the grass
- Visiting family
- Watching the sunset on the porch
- Listening to the birds

05 Trust God with the Gaps

Sometimes the goal feels far away. You're doing everything right, making steady progress, and it's still hard. Time stretches out and the path grows longer.

That's where faith steps in. God never asked you to carry the burden alone. He asked you to walk in obedience—and *He'll supply the rest* (Phil. 4:19).

Let joy be a part of your obedience, too.

Write down scripture verses and other motivating words that inspire you to stay true to your plan and vision. Write down ones that help you remember God, Jesus, and the Holy Spirit stand by your side and are with you all the way.

Keep any or all of the above lists where you can see them. When you feel deprived, review them instead of swiping your credit card. Standing at the top of your Rise Rich mountain will feel so much better than being buried under a mountain of debt.

 ## Rise Rich Exercise: Boss Up Your Budget

Saving without a budget is like trying to shoot a bullet in the dark. You might hit something, but probably not what you want.

Pull out the budget you started in chapter 2, which you now agree is very important to chart your financial course. It's time to start fine-tunning it. Following the tips below make it easier for you to take full command of your cash flow, so your savings grow with purpose. This helps you be intentional about staying in alignment with your money goals, without being too restrictive in the process of trying to manage your funds.

01 Use the 70/20/10 Rule, authored by Jim Rohn, a motivational speaker and business philosopher who maintains discipline with money is the foundation for wealth and character.

According to his rule, a good proportionate allotment of your total income can be broken down as follows:

- 70% of your income = Needs + Wants
- 20% = Savings
- 10% = Giving (tithe, charity, or community support)

If saving 20% feels like it's too much to save right now, flip the script:

- Start with 5%
- Increase 1% each month until you build the habit

02 Use Cash Envelopes for Problem Areas

In creating your budget, did you uncover any spending patterns or behaviors that surprised you? Are you overspending on food, rideshare, or fun? A trick to make you aware of overspending in areas where your flesh might get a little weak is to withdraw cash for those specific budget areas and give yourself a weekly allowance. When the money's gone, it's gone. Some people separate the allotments in envelopes to keep themselves honest.

03 Weekly Check-In = Wealthy Check-In

Spend ten minutes every Sunday night to:

- Check your bank balance
- Update your savings goals
- Celebrate any wins
- Reset if needed (there is no shame in this)

Checking in regularly on your financial standing is what grown folks do. Boss moves are made in quiet moments of discipline.

 **Journal Entry #3**
Write & Reflect: Money on a Mission

Take a quiet moment to reflect on the purpose behind your money moves. This is your space to connect your financial goals to what truly matters — your vision, your values, and your why. Answer each question with honesty and intention. Don't rush the process — let your thoughts flow freely.

Write from your heart, pray over your plans, and let purpose guide every dollar you direct.

01 If I could change my money situation in one major way over the next year, in what manner would that be?

....

....

....

02 What Rise Rich goal would make me feel proud, even if nobody else saw it?

....

....

....

03 What's one small step I can take this week toward that goal?

....

....

....

04 How can I build those small money-building steps into my weekly routine?

....

....

....

05 When I hit my next financial milestone, how will I reward
myself in a meaningful way?

....

....

....

Take One Step Closer to Your Richer Life

Wealth is more than what's in the bank. It's also peace, joy, freedom, and legacy. It is not a case of one or the other. You can
have discipline *and* delight. You can have plans *and* praise. You
can work *and* rest.

*"The blessing of the Lord makes rich, and He adds no sorrow
with it" (Prov. 10:22).*

Wealth isn't built in your wallet; it's built in your vision.
Start now. Program your GPS.

*"Commit to the Lord whatever you do, and he will establish
your plans" (Prov. 16:3 NIV).*

05 Maximizing Credit & Scores

Credit can be your best financial ally, or your worst enemy. For many first-time wealth builders, the first taste of financial freedom often comes in the form of a credit card offer tucked in the mail or pitched on a college campus. Swipe now, pay later sounds harmless...until later arrives with interest, late fees, and a balance that grows faster than your paycheck.

Too many people fall into credit traps because no one explained the rules of the game. Lenders know this. They market credit as convenience, but in reality, it's a test of discipline. Used wisely, credit can open doors, funding businesses, qualifying you for a home, even unlocking travel rewards and perks. Used recklessly, it can chain you to years of stress, damaged credit scores, and financial setbacks.

This chapter breaks down how credit really works, how to use cards as tools (not toys), and how to avoid the common traps that keep generations stuck in cycles of debt. By the end, you'll see that credit isn't something to fear, it's something to master. And once you do, you'll hold one of the most powerful keys to building lasting wealth.

My Story

I went wrong signing up for all my favorite store credit card offers. I racked up debt again and again with no understanding of the way credit worked. I took offers to save 20% on my purchase almost any time it was offered and didn't realize I was being bamboozled into paying the company back that discount if I carried my balance into the next month, and the next and the next as time went on. It's the downside of living in the moment, with no foresight of future goals.

I was religious about making sure I paid my bills on time. This came naturally to me, but by only paying the minimum payment, I actually paid thousands of dollars in interest and sent my debt-to-income ratio through the roof. I owed more than I was making. I was living off credit, getting nothing in return but high interest debt.

Then I tried to get crafty and work the system by applying for credit cards with 0% interest for a specific term. Once I got these cards, I'd transfer my balances from high interest credit cards to one of these. This cycle became a game of Three Card Monty that required a lot of mind power to keep track of.

However, my real downfall was that I still hadn't checked my spending problem. All my crafty strategy didn't prevent me from ending up in bankruptcy court. I was over-extended and needed to reset my financial state completely; I needed a fresh start with my money. That reset hit my credit score pretty hard, but I prepared myself to sacrifice that rating to gain some relief on the other side.

Let's talk about falling in the pit of "it was on sale!" for a moment.

Biblical Wisdom: First Corinthians 10:23 says, *"All things are lawful, but not all things are helpful."*

Let's keep it real: Sales can feel like a blessing. I don't know about you, but I couldn't wait to tell my friends:

- "It was 40% off!"
- "I saved $60!"
- "It was BOGO! How could I not buy it in all these colors?"

A lot of people convince themselves they're saving money when they're actually spending money unnecessarily. Discounts become an easy excuse to buy something that was never in the plan in the first place. Think about it: the store waves a sign that says *"40% OFF!"* and suddenly, instead of walking past, you're at the register buying shoes you didn't budget for.

That's not saving, that's spending with a coupon attached.

The trap is this: stores know that discounts trigger urgency. Phrases like *"limited time"* or *"only today"* are designed to make you feel like you'll miss out if you don't buy. But here's the reality: if you didn't need it before the sale, the discount doesn't make it necessary now. It's just a cheaper detour on the road to debt.

Street Truth: If you wouldn't buy it at full price, you probably don't need it at half price either.

When you've grown up watching every dollar, it feels smart to grab deals. We are taught to think:

- "If I don't get it now, I'll miss out."
- "People with money can afford this; I deserve nice things. too."
- "It's not even expensive. I got money for this now."

The wealthy don't buy things just because they're on sale; they buy when a purchase is aligned with their goals, their budget, and their vision. A discount might lower the price tag, but it doesn't change the fact that wasted money is wasted money.

Biblical Wisdom: Self-Control Is Greater Than Self-Indulgence

Proverbs 25:28 says, *"Like a city whose walls are broken through is a person who lacks self-control."*

That means every unplanned purchase, every emotional "I had to," is a crack in your financial foundation. A strong financial foundation is built on discipline, intentional spending, and a clear budget. Cracks appear when emotions, impulses, or outside influences pull you away from that structure. That fracture might look small at first—a $20 impulse purchase here, a "half-off" splurge there—but over time, those choices weaken your financial house. Instead of building wealth, you end up patching holes and slowing down your progress.

Sales aren't totally evil. They can aid your budget and make your money, and savings, go further. However, no price tag should own your peace.

When you are tempted to make an impulse or otherwise unplanned purchase, use this checklist before taking out your wallet. This is especially important when the item is "on sale."

That's when temptation can be at its strongest. Before you buy, ask yourself:

01 Was this already in my budget?
02 Would I still want this if it were full price?
03 Can I pay cash without using savings or credit?
04 Am I buying this to feel better? Is it a purchase because of boredom, stress, ego, etc.?
05 What goal or debt am I delaying if I buy this now?
06 Will this help me move forward to my Rise Rich vision or just make me feel good for a moment?
07 Can I walk away for twenty-four hours and be okay with buying it later?

If it's not a YES on all seven, it's a NO for now.
Take a picture of these questions and reference it while out shopping. Empowered choices will help you build your rich life.

Here's What I Learned

Spending and using credit should be done wisely and strategically. Credit is not free money. If used right, credit can accelerate your goals. If used wrong, it can delay your dreams. A good credit score gives access to better interest rates, higher limits, and more financial options.

Here are the key credit scoring factors you need to know. Being mindful of these factors, their weight, and the impact of each will ensure you maximize your credit scoring potential.

01 Payment history (35%) – Based On:

Do you pay your bills on time?

    a   Billing cycles are typically 28–31 days.

    b   Closing date (end of the cycle): This is the day your credit card company totals your charges, payments, fees, and interest for that period.

    c   Statement dates are usually the same as the closing date and will show all charges that were made in that cycle.

    d   Due date: This is usually 21–25 days after the cycle closes. If you pay the full balance by then, you avoid interest charged on any unpaid balance.

    e   Late payments, defaults, bankruptcies, and collections negatively affect your credit score.

    f   **At the very least, pay the minimum balance on time.**

02 Credit utilization (30%) – Based On:

How much of your available credit are you using?

    a   Try not to spend 100% of your available credit. This is called maxing out. Creditors look at your need to "max out" in a negative light, which I know seems contradictory in a sense, like why would you give me $X and not expect me to spend $X? A maxed-out card signals you're too heavily reliant on borrowed money. Lenders then think you're desperate for credit or struggling with managing your money.

    b   Using more than 30% of the credit available to you will lower your score. If you are using 10% or less, that will help increase your score.

03 Length of credit history (15%) – Based On:
How long have your accounts been open?

a   Try to keep your first well-paid account open for as long as you can; using it from time to time and paying off the balance. A longer, positive credit history improves your score.

b   One big mistake is paying off and closing long-standing, revolving credit accounts. You want those years/history to accumulate. Using them sparingly will stop creditors from closing your account due to prolonged inactivity.

04 Credit Mix (10%) – Based On:
How many credit vehicles do you have?

a   The mix of types of credit you have impacts your score, shifting it upward if the mix is diverse, or downward if it's just one or two. Types of credit include credit cards, auto loans, student loans, mortgages, and others. Lenders want to see that you can responsibly handle different forms of debt.

b   Having a mix of revolving (credit cards) and installment (loans) credit can boost your score. Revolving credit is a flexible credit line you can use repeatedly, up to a set limit, as long as you make at least the minimum payment each billing cycle. You can carry a balance, but you will be charged a variable interest rate that is usually higher than what it would be for installment loans. Installment loans are for a fixed amount repaid in set payments or installments over a specific period of time. Those payments are broken down into equal monthly payments to include interest, which is typically charged at a fixed rate and lower than revolving credit interest rates. Installment loans do not revolve, once you pay it off the account is closed.

05 New Accounts (10%) – Based On:
How many accounts have you opened or tried to open?

a   Don't let creditors arbitrarily run your credit. Instead, know the difference between a hard pull and a soft pull. A hard pull cannot be done unless you complete an application and agree to have a lender do so. A soft pull doesn't impact your score.

b   Hard pulls stay on your credit report for two years but only affect your credit score by lowering it by about five to ten points for about twelve months. I used to think I had a chance of being approved if I tried with another lender after being denied by one. I remember sending in one application after another when I was looking for credit cards that had balance transfer options. I applied and applied until I was approved for what ended up being an insignificant $500 or so. I hadn't realized how much damage I was doing to my credit score. Please note, the more denials you receive, the higher you increase how risky of a borrower you are perceived to be.

When it comes to rate shopping for loans, you have about a 14–45 day window (depending on the scoring model – Vantage or FICO, we'll discuss these in a bit) where inquiries are usually counted as one. This only applies when you are shopping for the same type of loan, like a mortgage, auto, or student loan. One or two hard pulls every couple years won't ruin your credit. The problem comes when you start looking like you're in financial distress to lenders by applying for multiple loans and/or loan types in a short period of time.

However, over time, the positive effect of responsible credit use outweighs the small dip from inquiries.

c   Soft pulls don't impact your score at all. It's a good idea to inquire about a soft pull for prequalification before submitting an application that would result in a hard pull. For example, soft pulls on your credit happen when:

- You check your own credit report or score.
- A lender researches for pre-approval.
- A company checks as part of their employment process.
- The financial institution behind your credit card does a credit review (they do this before increasing your limit).

Most banks and credit card companies report to the three credit bureaus: Equifax, Experian, and TransUnion. The process by which they do so generally looks like this:

- They report every 30–45 days.
- They may report to one, two, or all three bureaus.
- The reporting date is usually based on billing cycles (so, they may vary).
- Updates take a few days to impact your credit score at each bureau.

The banks and credit card companies report the following for every borrower:

- Account balance
- Payment status (late, on-time)
- Credit limit and usage
- Account date opened and closed
- Account type and terms

Ways Young Adults Can Build Good Credit

Your credit story begins the moment you step into financial independence. For young adults, every swipe, bill, and loan choice creates a trail that shapes opportunities for the future, whether it's renting an apartment, buying your first car, or even landing certain jobs. Building good credit early isn't just about numbers; it's about trust, discipline, and creating options for your rich life ahead. In this exercise, you'll learn simple, powerful steps to set your credit on the right track and avoid the traps that hold many back.

Here are fast and effective tips for young adults to build good credit from scratch:

01 Open a Secured Credit Card
Designed to help people build or rebuild their credit
- Requires a cash deposit as collateral, usually equal to your credit limit, which reduces the lender's risk, but it works just like a normal credit card
- Use it for small purchases and pay off in full monthly

Examples include: Discover It Secured, Capital One Platinum Secured, Chime Credit Builder Visa; Citi Secured Mastercard, OpenSky Secured Visa, Navy Federal nRewards Secured

02 Become an Authorized User (Parent/Guardian Endorsed)
- Ask a trusted family member to add you to their credit card
- Their positive history helps build your credit

03 Apply for a Starter Credit Card or Student Card
- Easier to qualify for when you have a limited or no credit history

- Use lightly and pay your full balance each month to build a solid credit history

04 Always Pay On Time
- Remember, payment history is the biggest factor of your FICO score (35%)
- Set up autopay or reminders to avoid late payments

05 Keep Balances Low
- Use less than 30% of your credit limit (under 10% is ideal)
- This shows responsible usage and helps your score increase

06 Monitor Your Credit
- Use free tools available at Credit Karma, Experian, etc.
- Check your reports for errors at AnnualCreditReport.com

07 Consider a Credit Builder Loan
- Offered by some banks or credit unions
- You make payments, and they report to the bureaus, building a good history

Use Credit to Your Advantage Wisely

 Biblical Wisdom: Proverbs 22:7 says, "The borrower is slave to the lender."

Credit can either be your worst enemy or one of your best tools. The difference isn't the card; it's how you use it. Too many people let credit control them, falling into traps of high interest, minimum payments, and impulse swipes. But when you flip the script, credit becomes a powerful lever: it can build your score, unlock opportunities, and even earn you rewards while you live within your means.

You must learn to put credit in its rightful place—under your control.

Here are some tips to use credit to your advantage:

01   Use Credit to Buy Appreciating Assets – Instead of using credit to fill voids or lack, like I did as a young adult, leverage credit to invest in assets that grow in value or generate income, such as real estate, a business, job certifications). Avoid using credit for depreciating items like luxury clothes, expensive cars, or impulse buys.

02   Balance Transfers – Use promotional 0% interest cards to pay off higher-interest debt or finance large purchases. Now, this should be done with strategic and intentional purpose of helping you get out of debt. I used this method as a bandaid to stop the bleeding on maxed out credit cards for as long as I could, and still I had a balance once the 0% offer expired in the six- or twelve-month timeframe. I ended up back in the same predicament. This is not strategic, it's hustling backwards! I should have focused on paying the full balance before the 0% interest rate offer expired. Set up a monthly payment schedule to achieve this mission.

03   Build Business Credit – Separate personal and business credit early on. Business credit helps you scale with less personal financial risk, and it opens doors to other sources of funding without draining your savings.

04 Finance Big Goals with a Plan – When understood and used with forethought, credit can help fund wealth-building ventures. Just remember, it is important to plan repayment before using credit, not after. Examples of expenditures of this nature include:

- Education or trade certifications
- Launching a side business
- Emergency needs (if savings aren't readily available)

05 Use Credit to Improve Cash Flow, Not Destroy It – If used correctly, credit can free up cash to invest, save, or grow your income. If misused, it traps you in high-interest debt cycles.

06 Don't Be Fooled by Store Credit Card Offers – When a cashier says, "Would you like 20% off today with our store card?" remember that 20% discount can cost you hundreds in interest if you don't pay off the balance right away. That "yes" could also lower your credit score with a hard inquiry and increase your temptation to overspend.

07 High Interest Rates Keep You Trapped – A 24% interest rate on a $1,000 balance means you could pay hundreds over time just in fees. Minimum monthly payments are meant to look easy while your balance payoff progression stands still. This is the revolving debt trap, and it catches so many of us as easily as spiders do flies in their webs.

08 Wisely Maximize Credit Card Rewards – For responsible spenders, rewards cards can work in your favor. However, this needs to be done intentionally. I recommend using the card to purchase things you'd purchase in a month typically, such as gas or groceries. Then, pay the balance in full monthly so you aren't paying interest. This way you are spending responsibly, helping your credit score, and earning rewards steadily. Today, I only use my American Express and only charge what I can pay off within thirty days. Doing this enhances my rich lifestyle because I use the reward points toward flights and hotel stays (travel is part of my Rise Rich happiness). I suggest you choose cards that match your rich lifestyle goals. Consider:

- Cash Back Cards: best for everyday purchases (groceries, gas, bills)
- Travel Rewards Cards: best if you fly, stay in hotels, or want points for free trips
- Rotating Bonus Cards: great if you can keep up with categories that change each quarter

I love looking at my AMEX reward points build like it's a breath of fresh air! To really take full advantage of card reward programs, you must FULLY UNDERSTAND what the benefits are and how they can be earned. Then, be intentional about maximizing credit card rewards (cash back, travel points) for purchases you'd make anyway. Only spending what you can pay off in full each month.

I cannot stress enough that you pay your balance in full each month. If you're carrying debt on these credit cards, the rewards are not worth it. Focus on getting debt-free first.

Rise Rich Exercise:
Get Your Credit Report (No Scores):

You can get a free copy of your credit report to review every year. It is important to be sure inaccurate information has not been reported to Equifax, Experian, and TransUnion. You can do this by logging into www.annualcreditreport.com. This site is the only official site authorized by federal law. There are many other websites that will charge you or solicit membership to allow access to your credit report. Nowadays, most financial institutions will provide one of the versions below free with an active bank account. You can also access free reports from the three credit bureaus individually or use one of the free sources provided below.

SOURCE	TYPE OF SCORE
Credit Karma	VantageScore (TransUnion & Equifax)
Credit Sesame	VantageScore (TransUnion)
Experian.com	FICO (Experian only)
Your Bank or Credit Card Issuer	Usually FICO or VantageScore

You might be asking yourself, what's the difference between a FICO and VantageScore? I'm glad you asked!

FICO: This report, developed by Fair Isaac Corporation, is based on six months of data (300–850 range), and is trusted by over 90 percent of top lenders. It can only be pulled for hard inquiries.

VantageScore: This report was developed by the credit bureaus Equifax, Experian, and TransUnion. It is based on one month of data. This is the score most seen and available to you online.

FICO and VantageScore weigh the data reported for your credit and loan accounts slightly differently, leading to you having slightly different credit scores between the two sources.

Journal Entry #4
Write & Reflect: Start Your Exit Plan

01 When have I used credit as a tool instead of a trap?

....

....

....

02 What credit habit do I need to change right now to align with my rich life goals?

....

....

....

Take One Step Closer to Your Richer Life

Review your credit cards this week. List your balances, interest rates, and due dates. Then, choose one move you can make immediately: paying more than the minimum, transferring a balance, or cutting back spending to free up payoff money.

06 Wise Saving

> **Biblical Wisdom:** Proverbs 21:20 says, *"Precious treasure and oil are in a wise man's dwelling, but a foolish man devours it."*

Most of us weren't taught to save. We were taught to survive.

When the money hit, when that paycheck came in, it had to go to rent, to food, to bills, or to whatever made the struggle feel a little lighter—even if it was just for the weekend.

But, that's the mindset of Hood life.

Real wealth, Rise Rich wealth, isn't only about making money. It's about keeping it and understanding how to keep it.

When you save, you're not just stacking cash; you're building courage. Saving with intention is a form of personal power. It's about freedom, focus, and future vision. You're making your future self proud. You're giving your children something to model. You're setting a standard for generations to come.

My Story

For many years, I took what banks in the Hood typically offered and what was common knowledge: a standard checking account to pay bills from and a savings account because it was paired with it. In the back of my mind, I constantly told myself I didn't make enough money to save. If I saved any money, it was temporary...I'd pull it anytime I wanted. I lost thousands of dollars over two decades because people in the Hood rarely possessed knowledge about high-yield savings accounts. How was I supposed to know to look for a higher interest yield? Interest yield wasn't even in my vocabulary... but lo and behold, some savings accounts pay you up to 4% on your money annually. For many years, ignorance resulted in me only earning a tenth of a percent annually... that loss adds up over time.

As I hope you understand from earlier chapters, you don't need six figures to start saving. You need vision, discipline, and a plan. This chapter shows you how to continue to develop all three. Your LifeStyle Tracker will show you when you are ready and with what amount you are able to dedicate to saving as you go. Trust the process!

Here's What I Learned

 Street Truth: If you don't save, you're one crisis from broke

Ask anyone who's been through a flat tire, a sick kid, one missed check – besides stressing you out, it can be financial chaos. Not because you're irresponsible, but because your budget had no cushion.

Saving is your shock absorber. It won't stop life from hitting, but it will soften the blow.

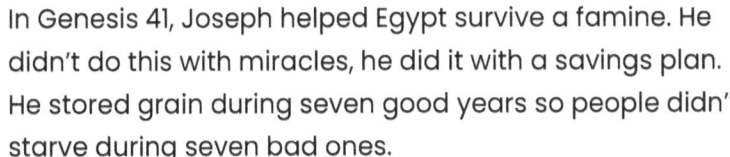

Biblical Wisdom: God Cares About Storehouses

In Genesis 41, Joseph helped Egypt survive a famine. He didn't do this with miracles, he did it with a savings plan. He stored grain during seven good years so people didn't starve during seven bad ones.

God blessed Joseph's wisdom because it saved lives.

Proverbs 6:6–8 tells us to learn from the work of the ant: *"It stores its provisions in summer and gathers its food at harvest."* That's not just ancient advice. That's wealth-building behavior.

You might be tempted to say all this saving is driven by fear. The ant is afraid of starving. Yet, that's not what the verse in Proverbs is teaching. It's about faith. You're not saying, "I am fearful. I don't trust God to provide." You're saying, "I trust Him enough to prepare." That's biblical wisdom and common sense working together.

And saving isn't selfish. It allows you to say yes to God when He tells you to give, to serve, or to build.

Rise Rich Exercise:
Build Saving Buckets

Most people save with no plan. They stash money "just in case," but they never connect their savings to a bigger picture. That's why saving feels boring, or worse, pointless. But when you save with purpose and intention, every dollar becomes a seed. You're not just stockpiling cash, you're building options, security, and freedom.

Biblical Wisdom: Luke 14:28 says, *"For which of you, intending to build a tower, sitteth not down first, and counteth the cost…"*

God calls us to "count the cost" before building. Saving with intention is exactly that: setting aside resources with a goal in mind so your future isn't left to chance.

This matters because when building a Rise Rich life with purpose, it makes the temporary sacrifice much easier. It's hard to skip a meal out to "just save." But it's easier if that money is fueling your dream home, your debt payoff, or your child's future. Once I established my rich life goals of living comfortable in retirement by age 55, see my children graduate college student loan free, and travel freely every quarter of the year, it was easy for me to say no to over or unnecessary spending. Being intentional like this also creates momentum. Instead of random deposits, you're aiming at something specific, like a down payment, emergency fund, or investment start-up.

The Three Buckets of Saving

01 Emergency Saving

Starting small with an emergency fund is the best approach because it builds momentum without pressure. Aiming for $500 to $1,000 first makes the goal feel achievable and gives you a quick win, which motivates consistency. Even a small cushion can prevent financial setbacks, keeping you from relying on credit cards when unexpected expenses arise. It also develops the habit of saving regularly, which strengthens financial discipline over time. Most importantly, having even a little money set aside creates a sense of control and peace of mind, while laying the foundation for eventually growing into a larger emergency fund that covers 3–6 months of expenses to meet the general rule of thumb. This will help you survive through real-life disruptions or unexpected expenses, such as:

- Loss of a job
- Car repairs
- Medical bills
- Broken major appliances

Rise Tip: Keep your emergency savings in a separate high-yield savings account so you're not tempted to spend it. I recommend finding one that allows access to your funds without much delay.

02 Opportunity Savings Bucket

This is your "get ahead" fund. It helps you say YES when good things come your way.

While an emergency fund protects you from setbacks, an opportunity savings bucket positions you for growth. This bucket isn't for crises; it's for possibilities. It gives you the flexibility to say yes when doors open, whether that's a business investment, a once-in-a-lifetime trip, a course that levels up your skills, or even a down payment for an opportunity that comes sooner than expected. Starting small here matters, too, because the goal is to create a pool of funds that fuels your future, not your fears. Saving with intention in an opportunity bucket shifts your mindset from scarcity to abundance. You're no longer just preparing for "what if something goes wrong," but also for "what if something goes right?"

Examples of Rise Rich opportunities that can create or build on your future success include:

- Starting a business
- Taking a class or pursuing a certification
- Investing in tools or skilled training
- Buying stocks or investing when the price is right

Rise Tip: Keep your emergency opportunity savings in a high-yield savings, a money market (for a slightly higher yield) or a short-term certificate of deposit (CD) account (if you don't need the money for 12–24 months and want a guaranteed rate of return).

03 Future & Freedom Saving Bucket

The future & freedom savings bucket is where you intentionally fund the life you're working so hard to create. Unlike an emergency fund that shields you from setbacks or an opportunity bucket that prepares you for doors opening, this account is about long-term rich dreams and lifestyle freedom. It could be early retirement, sending your kids to college debt-free, taking a year off to travel, or building a legacy project. Starting small here is powerful, because every deposit is a step toward buying back your time and designing the life you actually want to live. Saving with this bucket keeps you focused on the bigger picture; it's not just about money, it's about freedom, vision, and choices that align with your purpose. It includes setting aside money for:

- Retirement
- Buying a home
- Leaving something for your kids

Rise Tip: Keep your future & freedom savings in a retirement account (Roth IRA, 401(k), SEP IRA, etc.) for long-term wealth; a taxable brokerage account for freedom goals before retirement age (travel fund, early retirement, passion projects); and/

or a 529 Plan if saving specifically for children's education. These methods have served my rich life goals well. I started depositing just $25 per paycheck in my son's 529 Plan when he was about four years old. Had I not, the struggle to pay a private school tuition bill would have been a much heavier burden.

> *Proverbs 13:22 says, "A good man leaves an inheritance to his children's children." That's not solely about money; it's about mindset, strategy, and sacrifice now for your financial freedom later. This verse is another way of speaking about building generational wealth.*

Rise Rich Exercise:
How to Actually Start Saving

Biblical Wisdom: Saving Is Wise

Proverbs 21:20 says, *"The wise store up choice food and olive oil, but fools gulp theirs down."*

Saving can feel impossible when bills and debt already take up most of your paycheck. But here's the truth: saving isn't about the amount, it's about the habit. You don't wait until you have "extra" money to save. You create the habit now, even with a small amount, and let discipline grow into freedom. When you start small, such as $5, $10, or $25 at a time, you're not just moving money into an account. You're training yourself to prioritize your rich life goals and future. That small act builds momentum, shows God you're a faithful steward, and shifts your mindset from "I can't" to "I will."

This exercise guides you to set your first savings goal, automate your deposits, and celebrate progress, no matter how small. Remember: the goal isn't perfection, it's progress on purpose.

01 Make Saving Automatic

Making savings a habit is often easier when you have your bank to do it for you. Set up a weekly or monthly auto-transfer from your checking account. Even if you only start with $5, it adds up with time (This is a helpful way to save for retirement). What matters is the momentum you build.

02 Start with One Small Win

A small step is still a worthwhile step. Start saving with a small goal you consider a stretch but one that's possible to achieve. For example, challenge yourself to save $50 in seven days. Sell something, skip takeout, cut a bill. Then do it again. Small wins build big muscles. And don't forget to celebrate.

03 Save Unexpected Money

Sometimes you are blessed with some extra cash or an unexpected windfall. Did you get a tax refund? A little birthday cash? Your side hustle brought in more than you thought it would? When this fortunate situation happens, put at least part of that money into savings instead of blowing it all. Never treat extra money like bonus money. Treat it like seed.

Journal Entry #5
Write & Reflect: Saving on Purpose

01 What's held me back from saving in the past? Was it lack of income, fear, impulse spending, or something else? Is that still true today?

....

....

....

02 What would it feel like to have $1,000 saved and no need to touch it? Would that make anything in my life better or feel different?

....

....

....

03 What's one saving goal I can hit in the next 30 days? Be specific.

....

....

....

Take One Step Closer to Your Richer Life

Saving is not about being rich. It's about being ready. Ready for what's next. Ready to bless others. Ready for the life you were created to live.

However, seeing your progress is wonderful motivation for continuing your progress. I'm sure you've heard the saying "success begets success." Therefore, I'm providing you with the

Simple Savings Tracker below. Use this to track progress on any savings goal—whether it's your $1,000 emergency fund or long-term freedom savings. (Of course, feel free to create your own version.) I recommend taping this tracker to your fridge, wall, or journal. *Visibility keeps you accountable.*

Your Simple Savings Tracker

Goal Name:
....

Total Amount Needed:
....

Deadline Date:
....

WEEK	DATE	AMOUNT SAVED	TOTAL SO FAR	NOTES (HOW YOU SAVED)
1				
2				
3				
4				
5				
6				
7				

07 Break Free

Let's get one thing straight: Debt is not your identity. Debt is a situation, and situations can change. But in order to change the level of your debt, you've got to face it head-on. Not with guilt, not with fear, but with a plan. So, gear up to create your battle plan to break the crushing chains of debt and move toward financial and emotional freedom.

My Story

Removing the foot of oppression, called the debt trap, from me and my husband's back took a huge leap of faith along with major strategy, focused discipline, and execution. Under a one-year plan, we wanted to pay off all debt and re-position ourselves in a living situation that decreased our monthly overhead. There were several self-inflicted increases we wanted to reduce or eliminate entirely. For example, we wanted to rid ourselves of private school bills and live in an area with less day-to-day driving (saving on gas, parking, and commuting in general). We decided to use our home to attack our debt as well. We rented our house, which increased our monthly income because the rent covered the mortgage and left us some remaining. Plus, we sold mostly everything in it and moved in with in-laws for a year.

These were all game changers, and we saw major results in a that year period. We paid off over $40,000 in debt, reduced our monthly overhead by $1,000, increased our income by $2,000, and built a five-figure savings account.

This new start was so very refreshing and started us on the journey of becoming debt free. There was more to do, however. We had to continue with faith, strategy, discipline, and execution. It was not time to stop our efforts.

I turned in my car. I really didn't need it since I now lived in an area with easy access. I could walk or use public transportation to reach just about anything or anywhere I needed, except to visit family, so my husband and I shared one car. We purchased my son a used car for $1,500 to primarily travel to and from school for about 2 years. I took over driving this vehicle when he went off to college and still leverage the use of it in order to put off paying a car note. This saved me over $10,000 a year, and more than $51,000 over the past 5 years.

These major money moves required major shifts in my family's life. Renting out our home to generate passive income meant we needed to arrange living with family for one year. Moving to another city reduced our cost of living, but it came with the disruption a move and settling into a new area brings. Our vow to convert to cash-and-carry only and never again be burdened with credit card debt required a major lifestyle and mindset change. These moves all happened in under 2 years, and we continue to fine-tune our plans in ways that promote financial growth, freedom, and peace of mind.

 Street Truth: Credit Is Easy – Freedom Takes Work

Debt feels normal in today's world.

- Student loans? "Everybody has them."
- Credit cards? "Just pay the minimum."
- Buy now, pay later? "It's okay to treat yourself; you deserve it."

But that's the story of Hood Life. That's the accepted fact that normal is broke. But broke isn't where your story ends. That's not where you are going to settle. Not when you have plans set to Rise Rich in all ways of your life.

Biblical Wisdom: God Doesn't Want You Bound

Romans 13:8 says, *"Let no debt remain outstanding, except the continuing debt to love one another."*

This Bible verse reminds us that debt is not God's design for our lives. Financial debt keeps us tied to lenders and limits our freedom. Every unpaid bill or loan is a weight that prevents us from walking fully in our purpose. God wants us to live free—free to give, free to serve, and free to love without financial chains holding us back.

The only "debt" God approves of is love. Love is the one thing you can never finish paying because it's meant to overflow daily into the lives of others. That means while we should work diligently to pay off financial debts, we should never stop paying the "debt" of kindness, generosity, forgiveness, and compassion.

Before you can attack debt, you need to know the type of debt you're facing. **Bad debt** is borrowing that drains your money without building any long-term value. This includes high-interest credit cards, payday loans, or financing items that lose value immediately, like clothes, gadgets, or luxury items bought on impulse. Bad debt traps you in cycles of payments and interest that steal from your future. **Neutral debt** doesn't necessarily harm or help, it includes things like car loans or small personal loans. While necessary in some cases, neutral debt should be approached carefully because, while it doesn't necessarily build wealth, it can provide stability or convenience. **Strategic debt**, on the other hand, is borrowing that positions you for growth and future gain. This could be a student loan that leads to higher earning potential, a mortgage that builds home equity, or a business loan that funds expansion. Strategic debt is not about taking on loans recklessly, as previously discussed; it's about using credit as a tool to advance your goals and create long-term freedom. The key difference between these three is whether debt takes money from your pocket, simply passes through, or eventually puts more money back in.

TYPE	EXAMPLES	STREET SMART TAKE
Bad Debt	Credit cards, payday loans, rent-to-own situations	High interest, no asset. Work to get rid of it fast
Neutral Debt	Student loans, car loans, debts with low interest	Not ideal, but manageable if paid wisely
Strategic Debt	Home mortgage, business loans	Can build wealth if used with wisdom, but a risk if mismanaged

Boss Move Debt Payoff Strategies

There are two main ways to effectively pay off credit card debt: the **Snowball Method** and the **Avalanche Method**. The Snowball Method, coined by financial guru Dave Ramsey, is where I began my own journey. About five years ago, I enrolled in Dave Ramsey's financial coaching certification program, not because I planned to coach others, but because I needed to help myself and my family. Looking back, it was one of the best investments I ever made. That $4,000 investment didn't just buy me information; it gave me a complete mindset shift and ultimately led me to a debt-free lifestyle. The Snowball Method is a powerful way to gain momentum because you start by listing your debts from smallest to largest. You pay the minimums on all of them, but you throw every extra dollar you can at the smallest balance. Once that debt is gone, you roll that payment into the next smallest, and the cycle continues. The biggest benefit is motivation, you see progress fast, and that fuels you to keep going.

The second approach is the **Avalanche Method**, which focuses not on balance size but on interest rates. Credit cards often carry very high APRs, sometimes as steep as 29.99%, and the Avalanche Method helps you save the most money over time. To use it, you list your debts from the highest interest rate to the lowest and focus on paying extra toward the one costing you the most in interest. Once that's paid off, you roll that payment into the debt with the next highest rate and continue until all debts are cleared. The greatest advantage of this strategy is that it minimizes the total interest you pay, making it the more cost-efficient option in the long run.

Both strategies work. It's not about choosing the "perfect" method, but about choosing the one that keeps you moving forward. Debt payoff is less about perfection and more about progress. The key is to stay consistent and committed, no matter which path you take, because freedom comes from momentum and persistence.

Rise Rich Exercise:
Free Up Cash for Debt

One of the biggest barriers to debt freedom isn't lack of desire, it's lack of cash flow. The good news is, you probably have more money available than you think; it's just hiding in habits, subscriptions, and impulse spending. In this exercise, you'll take an honest look at where your money is going each month and identify small shifts that can create big results. The goal isn't to deprive yourself but to realign your spending so that every dollar aligns with a rich mission. By freeing up even $50 to $200 a month, you'll accelerate your debt payoff journey and get one step closer to your rich lifestyle.

Track your spending for the past 30 days, highlight at least three expenses you can reduce or eliminate, and redirect that money toward debt. Progress happens when you stop letting money slip away unnoticed and start commanding it with purpose. Here are a few tips to keep in mind:

- Cut what's not helping you: app subscriptions, fast food, streaming services, luxury expenses
- Pause unnecessary spending and put "wants" on hold. Ask yourself if it's an absolutely crucial "need" or just something "nice to have."
- Sell something: old clothes, gadgets, furniture, collectible sneakers. Turn your clutter into cash.
- Side hustle it: Use the extra money ONLY to pay off debt or build savings

Do NOT Do This While Paying Off Debt

- Don't stop saving completely. Even $10 a month builds discipline.
- Don't ignore your credit score. Pay your bills on time and check your report frequently.
- Don't fall for "debt relief" scams. You don't need a company to fix your situation; you will work your plan.

Journal Entry #6
Write & Reflect: Fight Your Way Out of the Trap

01 How do I feel when I look at my debt total—ashamed, overwhelmed, determined, numb?

....

....

....

02 What would freedom from debt feel like in my life?

....

....

....

03 Which debt should I attack first, and which method will I use?

....

....

....

Take One Step Closer to Your Richer Life

Progress beats perfection. Choose a payoff method, stick to it, and keep moving. Remember, the best debt payoff plan is the one you'll actually follow! Use the quick steps below to choose and execute a debt relief method that fits you best.

STEP 1: Know Your Numbers

List every debt you owe, including the balance, minimum payment, and interest rate. This gives you a full picture of where you stand and helps you decide on the best strategy.

STEP 2: Choose Your Method

- If you need **quick wins and motivation**, choose the **Snowball Method** (tackle the smallest balance first).
- If you want to **save the most money long-term**, choose the **Avalanche Method** (tackle the highest interest rate first).

STEP 3: Make a Plan

Commit to paying the minimum on all debts and direct all extra cash to the target debt (the one chosen by your method). Write this down and treat it like a non-negotiable bill.

STEP 4: Free Up Extra Cash

Review your spending for hidden leaks, such as unused subscriptions, eating out, and impulse buys, and redirect those dollars toward your target debt. Even $50 to a$100 a month accelerates progress.

STEP 5: Execute Consistently

Every time you pay off one debt, roll that payment into the next debt on your list. Keep the snowball or avalanche moving until all debts are gone. Success begets more success.

STEP 6: Celebrate and Stay Focused

Acknowledge each victory to keep your momentum alive. But don't stop, once debt is gone, keep redirecting that cash into savings, investing, or other rich life goals.

08 Rise Within, Then Extend

You don't need to wait for a mega millions lottery miracle! God has already given you something to multiply. Building true wealth requires more than just managing what comes in and what goes out. It's about learning to multiply what's already in your hands. The Bible reminds us of the parable of the talents, where those who invested wisely saw increase, while the one who buried his gift lost even what he had. The same is true for us. If we only hold onto what we have, fear and scarcity will keep us stuck. But, when we put our resources – our money, skills, and opportunities – to work with intention, we create growth that carries us beyond survival into freedom. This chapter shows you practical and purposeful ways to multiply what you have through saving in the right places, investing wisely, and recognizing opportunities to build wealth that lasts.

 Biblical Wisdom: Proverbs 21:5 says, *"The plans of the diligent lead to profit as surely as haste leads to poverty."*

In other words, fast money fades. Quick fixes, shortcuts, and get-rich-quick schemes usually end in loss. God honors diligence, discipline, and stewardship, the slow-and-steady work that compounds over time.

On the streets, everybody's chasing fast money. But fast money slips through your fingers just as fast as it comes. Multiplied money, the kind that grows through wise saving, investing, and reinvesting, sticks. It builds over time and creates a foundation you can pass on.

 Street Truth: The choice is yours – chase a quick bag or build lasting wealth.

A Hood Rich mindset can trick you into believing you lack access, but the reality is there's likely a lack in awareness of what's in front of you that you can use to your advantage. I realized this over time. And, when I did, the direction of my rich life journey became crystal clear.

My Story

In my federal civilian career, I quickly realized my income would only grow in small, fixed increments each year. That reality pushed me to chase side hustles to supplement my earnings. I tried several, mostly multi-level marketing programs, and, at first, the excitement of quick profits gave me a rush. But, once the sales to friends and family slowed down and the real work of selling to strangers began, I lost interest.

Looking back, I see that I wasn't leaning into my strengths. I was simply chasing the promise of money. I was intrigued by the "potential" but blind to the limits because my willingness to "sell, sell, sell" only extended as far as my comfort zone. Each time I jumped into one of these ventures, I ended up feeling stuck in yet another cycle I never wanted to be in.

What I didn't know then, but understand now, is that wealth isn't about chasing quick profits. Instead, it's about discipline, intention, and using what's already in your hands. Those failed ventures taught me an important truth: money without purpose will always run out, but money tied to vision multiplies. And that's the lesson I want to resonate with you.

 Street Truth: Budgeting Alone Won't Make You Rich.

After everything this book has taught about budgeting, this street truth might sound confusing at first because you can't out-save a low income forever. Certainly, budgeting and saving are powerful tools that help you control your money, stop over-spending, and build good habits. However, if your income is too low, there will always be a limit to how much progress you can make. You can cut back and save faithfully, but eventually you'll hit a wall. When there's nothing left to trim, the only way forward is to grow your income.

That's why financial freedom is not just about saving more; it's about earning more. Your budget gives every dollar a pur-pose, but increasing the value of your income multiplies the impact of that budget and your lifestyle. At some point, you have to shift from just cutting back to leveling up. That doesn't mean grinding nonstop; it means making smarter choices with your resources. For example, instead of eating out every day, you might stretch $20 of groceries into meals that last all week. Instead of stressing about buying a new car, you keep your older ride well-maintained, so it carries you further without draining your pockets. The same principle applies to hustling; rather than chasing every quick-money scheme that comes along, you focus on the one skill you already have, like braiding, baking, or cutting hair, and you build that steadily. Even with money management, being intentional means resisting the urge to blow a tax refund or lump sum on things you don't need instead of putting some toward savings, paying down a bill, and still leaving a little to enjoy. And sometimes it's about community – sharing rides, cooking together, or pooling resources with family so the weight doesn't all fall on one person. In short, being intentional isn't about exhausting yourself chasing more, it's about stretching what you have, moving smarter, and using every dollar with purpose.

 Biblical Wisdom: God Blesses the Work of Your Hands

So many people shy away from wanting more income because they fear it looks like greed. But there's a clear difference between greed and stewardship. Greed hoards; it chases money for the sake of status, excess, or selfish desire. Stewardship multiplies; it takes what God has already placed in your hands and grows it with purpose.

In the Parable of the Talents (Matthew 25:14–30), the servants who multiplied what they were given were called "faithful" and "trusted with more." The one servant who buried his talent out of fear was called "wicked and lazy." This story isn't about chasing riches, it's about responsibility. When you multiply your skills, your influence, and your income, you're not just providing for yourself, you're creating overflow that blesses your family, community, and even generations to come.

In real life, that might look like taking your skill for braiding hair and turning it into a side hustle, or using your creativity to build an online store, or asking for the raise you've earned instead of settling for less. Each act of multiplying is an act of stewardship. It honors God by not letting your gifts go to waste.

When we shift our mindset from *"I just need enough to get by"* to *"I have enough to build, bless, and leave a legacy,"* we align our finances with God's vision. Multiplying what you have is not about greed, it's about growth, responsibility, and honoring the One who gave you the resources in the first place.

Rise Rich Exercise:
You Are Your Greatest Asset

For your exercise, read through this three-part framework and choose one item you can do to add to your income with the abilities or resources you already have. This framework centers on personal strengths and talents unique to you.

Part 1 – Income: Make More Without Selling Your Soul

"All hard work brings a profit" (Prov. 14:23).

Focus on one income stream you can grow quickly with your current time, talents, and tools. While more than one of these possibilities may be an option, don't chase every opportunity. Doing that will exhaust you and keep you from enjoying the life you are aiming to have.

Ways to Increase Income:

- Ask for a raise at your current job (come with factual records of exceptional performance and unsolicited

feedback, not just hopes. If you aren't performing at this level, start today!)
- Take on overtime or bonus shifts for the short term
- Learn a new skill online (take advantage of free or low-cost platforms like Coursera, YouTube, Skillshare, etc.)
- Start a side hustle based on what you can do now
  - Cleaning, tutoring, rideshare, food delivery, graphic design, reselling items, childcare, etc.
- Turn a hobby into income (braiding hair, baking, crafting, photography)

Part 2 – Skills: Grow What Makes You Valuable

"Do you see a man skilled in his work? He will stand before kings" (Prov. 22:29).

The more skilled you are, the more options you'll have, and the more you can charge. Adding to your knowledge base never hurts, plus it makes you a more desired employee or attractive job applicant.

Remember: Every skill you gain becomes a seed that can grow into income, impact, or influence.

Ways to Grow One's Skills:

- Pick a skill to grow this month (sales techniques, software program, social media, customer service, a new language, etc.)
- Invest thirty minutes a day in learning and practicing the skill you're trying to grow
- Find a mentor or someone more skilled than you in that area and ask questions

- Offer your help in exchange for experience (be a volunteer, intern, or shadow for free)

Part 3 – Value: Show Up Like You're Worth More

When it comes to growing your skills – and by extension, your income – your presence, attitude, and consistency are as important as the skill itself. Showing up matters because opportunities often come to the ones who are simply present and available. Your attitude matters because people often hire, refer, or support someone they trust and enjoy working with over another who has slightly more talent because that person lacks humility or positivity. And your consistency matters most of all, because skill without discipline fades, but steady practice compounds into mastery.

In the long run, it's not always the person with the rawest talent who wins, it's the one who keeps showing up with the right spirit and the willingness to grow a little more each day. This is how you multiply what you have: by being present when it counts, carrying yourself with an attitude that reflects excellence, and staying consistent until your gifts make room for you.

You don't need a title to act like a leader. You don't need a degree to deliver excellence. You only need a willing heart.

Elevate Your Value by:

- Being reliable and on time. This demonstrates your wealth behavior.
- Communicating clearly and respectfully. Once more, this demonstrates your wealthy aptitude.
- Going the extra mile – people notice the effort and attention. When I worked at Nordstrom, this was one of the training mechanisms we used to generate return customers.

- Carrying yourself with confidence. There's no need to flex, just own your space and be comfortably authentic while reading the room and being mindful of the appropriate behavior in that place and time.

Journal Entry #7
Write & Reflect: Level Up

01 What's one skill I already have that I can use to make more money?

....

....

....

02 What talents am I hiding out of fear, doubt, or comfort?

....

....

....

03 What can I do this week to grow in value—either at work, in my business, or in my community?

....

....

....

Take One Step Closer to Your Rich Life

Don't Chase the Bag , Build the Gift

The money will come. But the goal is to multiply your ability, not just your cash. Because once you multiply you, increase your abilities, skills, and talents, no one can take that from you. Not a job loss. Not the economy. Not the haters. You are the asset. And when God multiplies what's in your hands, no system or statistic can stop it.

"Your gift will make room for you and bring you before great men" (Prov. 18:16).

Bonus Section: Fast Money Isn't Freedom – The Truth About Lottery & Gambling

"Wealth gained hastily will dwindle, but whoever gathers little by little will increase it" (Prov. 13:11 ESV).

When money is tight, quick fixes look really attractive. Scratch-offs. Slots. Sports bets. Lotto dreams. We think:

- "This might be my only shot."
- "It's just a few dollars to play."
- "What if I actually win?"

But here's the truth: lottery and gambling are not wealth-building tools – they're traps. Especially for people starting from struggle. They are not a dependable way of building real wealth.

Don't chase the cash promises of fast money. Your Rise Rich vison is building something that lasts. Fast money feels good for a moment. Real wealth gives you peace every day.

CATEGORY	FAST MONEY	REAL WEALTH
Source	Lottery, gambling, scams, shady deals	Skills, business, wise investing, career growth
Speed	Quick, but short-lived	Slow, but sustainable
Risk	High, and you usually lose	Low to medium, though is a strategic smart risk
Control	Depends on chance or someone else	You control your growth and choices
Impacts on mindset	Emotional highs / lows, desperation	Confidence, peace, long-term vision
Biblical alignment	Based on greed and chance	Based on stewardship and faithfulness
Legacy	None, it disappears fast	Long-term, can change your family tree
Typical outcome	Regret, debt, addiction, broken trust	Stability, growth, opportunities
End result	Emptiness, starting over	Freedom, options, overflow

 Street Truth: The Game Is Rigged

Let's do the math.

- The odds of winning the lottery?
- 1 in 292 million. It's true: you're more likely to be hit by lightning, twice.
- The lottery targets low-income communities more than any other group.
- Studies show the poorest neighborhoods spend the *most* on tickets, and those communities, and the people in them, remain stuck in this behavior.
- Gambling creates false hope and real losses. Even small bets add up. (Many people are shocked when they enter these spends in their budget.)

The house always wins. Because the house has a system, and you're not in it.

 Biblical Wisdom: God Doesn't Bless Greed or Chance

The Bible never supports gambling. Why? Because it's built on:

- Lust for fast money without work
- Risking what you can't afford to lose
- False hope in luck instead of faith in God

Proverbs 28:22 says, "A stingy man is eager to get rich and is unaware that poverty awaits him."

God blesses *diligence*, not desperation. When famine struck Egypt in Genesis 41, Joseph didn't scramble in desperation because he had already worked diligently for seven years, storing up grain during seasons of abundance because of the wisdom God gave him. When the hard times came, Egypt (and even surrounding nations) had provision though his planning. Joseph shows us that desperation waits until the crisis hits, but diligence prepares in advance. God blessed his consistency, foresight, and stewardship, not panic moves when it was too late.

Desperation looks like waiting until the rent is due to figure out how to come up with money, or swiping a credit card because you didn't plan. Diligence is setting aside a portion of each paycheck, paying bills on time, and being faithful in small things. One creates stress; the other creates stability.

 ### *Rise Rich Exercise:*
Play Your Own Lottery

The heart of the lottery is winning money. It feels really good to have surprise cash hit your doorstep. But there are other ways to create "surprise money" for yourself. All it takes is a change in mindset and dedication.

Your exercise is to try one of the ideas below. And remember, doing your best is more important than doing the challenge perfectly.

IDEA 1

Put your lottery money in a jar every time you'd normally buy a ticket. Then count and track the amount daily or weekly. I know this might hurt if you frequently pray to win a $100 box but stay the course so you can see the REAL NET BALANCE of your lottery spending.

Now, here's the tough part—discipline yourself to not touch the money adding up in the jar! This is not free money to spend.

This is money you are going to invest in yourself or add to that month's income.

IDEA 2

Challenge yourself to build a year-end surprise saving bucket. Whether you have a few dollars or a larger amount of cash, the success of this challenge only requires consistency and discipline.

On whatever schedule you set and with whatever amount of money you earmark, transfer it to an account you're not likely to touch. It can add up like this:

Weekly to Yearly Savings Examples

$15 / week = $780 / year

$20 / week = $1,040 / year

$25 / week = $1,300 / year

$50 / week = $2,600 / year

Daily to Yearly Savings Examples
(great for "coffee money" or "fast food swaps")

$1 / day = $365 / year

$2 / day = $730 / year

$3 / day = $1,095 / year

$5 / day = $1,825 / year

Monthly to Yearly Savings Examples

$25 / month = $300 / year

$50 / month = $600 / year

$100 / month = $1,200 / year

$250 / month = $3,000 / year

Redirecting these funds to fuel a rich life goal to build an emergency fund, seed money for a business, a weekend get-away, or a home upgrade might be closer than you think.

IDEA 3

Invite your family to join you in a No Spend Days challenge. It works just like its name says. For however long a period of time you want, think week(s) to a month, see how many days in a row you can go without spending money on non-essential items. Before starting, create a list together of acceptable non-essential items.

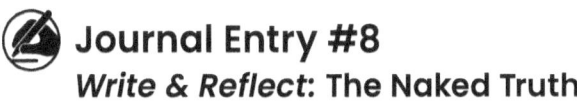 **Journal Entry #8**
Write & Reflect: **The Naked Truth**

01 How much have I spent in my life on lottery, scratch-offs, or gambling?

....

....

....

02 What could I have built with that money?

....

....

....

Take One Step Closer to Your Rich Life

You're already holding the ticket. The real lottery is the one you have already won.

- You woke up today.
- You have a mind to fill with knowledge.
- You have skills to grow.
- You have access to wisdom from many sources.

That's your win. Now multiply it.

09 Rich Is More than Money

"I came that they may have life and have it abundantly"
– (John 10:10 ESV).

Building wealth doesn't mean you have to live in misery while you wait for "someday." You don't have to live like a monk or a person who is broke to make progress with your finances. Wealth isn't just about money – it's about the life you're creating with it.

My Story

Anyone who knows me is fully aware that when I lock in on a goal, my focus is unshakable. But those same people also know I'm intent on enjoying life. For me, balance isn't optional, it's survival. Without it, I risk burning out, snapping under pressure, or letting stress steal the joy from the very life I'm working so hard to build. Taking breaks and making space for enjoyment is how I keep my mind clear and my spirit grounded, even when life behind the scenes feels chaotic.

As I grew older, I realized that rest and fun weren't luxuries, they were necessities. I began to prioritize couples' vacations, family trips, and intentional time with loved ones, not as an escape, but to recharge and reset. That balance allows me to return to my goals with fresh energy, sharper focus, and a healthier perspective. Balanced living also taught me a bigger truth: success is hollow if you're too exhausted to enjoy it. The hustle matters, but so does laughter, love, and stillness.

When we budget time and money for joy, not just bills and responsibilities, we honor the whole picture of life. That's what balanced living is about: building wealth and discipline while also creating space for peace, connection, and experiences that remind us why we're doing the work in the first place.

 Street Truth: Wealth Goes Beyond Numbers, It's Experiences, Too

A Hood Rich mentality leads you to easily falling into the trap of thinking:

- "Once I hit a certain number, I'll be happy."
- "I'll enjoy life after I pay off this debt."
- "I'll relax when I reach my financial goals."

Living with this mindset, you're losing sight of why you're building wealth in the first place. Wealth doesn't just buy you a house or a car. It buys you choices. Choices to live, gain experience, and grow along the way. The Rise Rich Life is not about waiting for things to get better; it's about learning to enjoy what you have while you build. Applying discipline to reach your vision of wealth should not feel like a punishment for accruing debt.

 Biblical Wisdom: Be Present and Enjoy Your Blessings

Ecclesiastes 3:13 says, "That each of them may eat and drink, and find satisfaction in all their toil—this is the gift of God."

God calls us to be grateful and enjoy the work we put in, not just fixate on the end goal. Financial freedom is a marathon, not a sprint. In other words, expect your journey to take time. Just as your debt pile didn't form overnight, your pile of wealth isn't going to either.

 **Rise Rich Exercise:**
Get Rich and Still Enjoy Life

It's important to celebrate the small wins, enjoy the journey, and share moments with those you love as you run your financial race. To not forget to do this, include space in your budget for enjoying life. As your assignment, add a realistic amount of funds to your budget now, selecting from the tips below.

01 Budget for Fun

A big part of enjoying life is knowing you can afford it. This advice is not about overspending. Instead, it's about planning for the things that bring personal joy. What fun can you realistically include in your budget?

- Prioritize your enjoyment. Whether it's eating out, a weekend getaway, or movie nights, allocate money to things you'll look forward to. Call this your "fun fund."
- Avoid guilt by making sure these happy items and experiences are in the plan.
- Don't neglect experiences that keep you connected, such as connecting with family, friends, and hobbies.

02 Be Smart About Treats Without Overdoing It

You can still enjoy life without throwing your entire budget out the window. Fun, joy, excitement, and happiness can be added to your world without costing a fortune.

- Stay local: Explore free or low-cost activities in your area, such as hiking, picnics in the park, art gallery tours.
- Buy experiences, not things. Examples include a guided road trip, a class, a concert. These memories last longer than material things.
- Do what's within your budget. Don't let "keeping up with the Joneses" derail your progress. Are first-class tickets that important?

03 Celebrate Small Wins

Every milestone in your financial journey is a reason to celebrate, whether it's paying off a debt, building your emergency savings, or hitting a weekend get-away vacation goal.

- Treat yourself within your budget: A meal at your favorite restaurant, a day off, a new book, or a small luxury that brings you joy.
- Share the love: Celebrate with friends or family with a potluck. Sometimes the best memories are the ones made together.

Journal Entry #9
Write & Reflect: EnRICH Your Life

01 What brings me joy outside of money? How can I bring more of this into my life?

02 How can I incorporate fun into my financial goals without feeling guilty?

....

....

....

03 What small win can I celebrate this week?

....

....

....

Take One Step Closer to Your Rich Life

Living life with enjoyment is part of the Rise Rich wealth building process. The two should not be separated because it results in burnout and falling off the path toward your wealth goal. Building wealth isn't about achieving the "perfect life; it's about creating a life you can enjoy along the way.

When you integrate fun, joyful experiences, and meaning into your journey, it doesn't feel like a sacrifice, it feels like progress. And that makes the path to financial freedom much more fulfilling.

"The blessing of the Lord brings wealth, without painful toil for it" (Prov. 10:22).

10 Intentional Investing

"Invest in seven ventures, yes, in eight; you do not know what disaster may come upon the land" (Ecclesiastes 11:2 NIV).

Investing isn't just about the stock market, it's about how you use every resource you have: money, time, skills, and even protection tools like insurance. Each type of investment carries its own benefits and risks, but all of them share one principle: you spend something today to build something greater tomorrow. Every dollar, every decision, every hour is either growing something or wasting something. The key is to make sure your investments, whether financial, personal, or spiritual, are aligned with your vision for a rich life. In this chapter, I lay some groundwork on all the various ways you should be intentional about how you invest your time and money.

For many people, financial investing feels intimidating. The terms can sound like another language – stocks (ownership in a company), bonds (loans to companies or governments), exchange-traded funds (ETFs), dividends (profits shared with investors), and individual retirement accounts (IRAs) – and that can make beginners freeze before they even take the first step. It can also feel confusing because there are so many options: should you buy individual stocks, invest through an online app, or focus on long-term retirement accounts like a 401(k) or Roth IRA? With all these choices, it's easy to believe that one wrong move could ruin everything. And for some, it just feels too hard to learn – especially if you grew up in an environment where investing wasn't discussed or if money already felt tight. It's easy to think investing is only for the wealthy or for people with advanced degrees in finance.

The truth, however, is much simpler. Investing doesn't require perfection, wealth, or a degree. It requires a willingness to start small, stay consistent, and learn as you go. Even the best investors began as beginners, and what separated them wasn't their knowledge on day one, it was their decision to take the first step. This chapter will show you how to break down the intimidation factor, simplify the confusion, and begin investing money and time with intention and confidence.

Here are the key areas of investing defined with a snapshot of pros and cons to consider. Understanding each of these in detail requires consultation with a licensed financial advisor, so I'll stay in my lane with exposing you with this general information. Dig deeper where you feel the need to rise.

01 Stock Market Investments
Definition: Buying shares of a company or a group of companies through stocks, mutual funds, ETFs, or index funds.
Pros: Long-term growth potential, compounding returns, easy to start with apps or brokers, passive if diversified.
Cons: Market volatility, potential losses if you panic-sell, requires patience.

02 Retirement Accounts
Definition: Accounts designed to save and invest for retirement, often with tax benefits, such as 401(k)s, IRAs, Roth IRAs, etc.
Pros: Tax advantages, long-term growth, employer matches (which equals free money).
Cons: Penalties for early withdrawals, limited contribution amounts each year.

03 Real Estate

Definition: Buying property to live in, rent, or invest in through REITs (real estate investment trusts).

Pros: Builds equity, generates rental income, hedges against inflation.

Cons: High upfront costs, ongoing maintenance, potential for vacancies or market downturns.

04 Business & Entrepreneurship

Definition: Starting or owning a business, side hustle, or franchise.

Pros: Unlimited income potential, control over your time, tax write-offs.

Cons: Risk of failure, inconsistent income, requires discipline and effort.

05 Bonds

Definition: Lending money to a government or company in exchange for regular interest payments.

Pros: Lower risk than stocks, predictable income, good for diversification.

Cons: Lower returns than stocks, can lose value if interest rates rise.

06 Commodities & Alternatives

Definition: Physical goods like gold, silver, oil, or newer options like cryptocurrency.

Pros: Can hedge against inflation, growth potential in certain markets.

Cons: High volatility, require specialized knowledge, risky if speculative.

07 Education & Skills
Definition: Investing in yourself through school, certifications, courses, or coaching.
Pros: Increases earning potential, builds confidence, lifelong value.
Cons: Upfront cost of time and money, requires follow-through to see results.

08 Time
Definition: How you intentionally spend hours to build skills, relationships, and wealth.
Pros: Completely within your control, compounding effect if used wisely, priceless for health and peace.
Cons: Easy to waste on distractions, can't be replaced once it's gone.

09 Life Insurance (Whole & Term)
Definition: A financial product that pays your beneficiaries upon death; some policies also build cash value.
Pros: Protects your family's future, whole life can grow savings, tax advantages in some cases.
Cons: Premium costs, whole life can be complex and expensive, requires commitment.

10 Giving & Legacy
Definition: Investing in others through tithes, donations, or setting up trusts for future generations.
Pros: Creates spiritual, emotional, and community returns; leaves a lasting impact.
Cons: No direct financial return, requires faith that giving multiplies in non-financial ways.

My Story

After I had my son, I learned a little about how credit could work for me, but I still felt the burden of paying off my student loans. I used to sit at my desk and wonder what my bottom line would look like if I hadn't had that payment requirement. I could only go into forbearance (when a lender allows you to temporarily pause or reduce your loan payments for a set period of time because of financial hardship), so many times. However, you know the time eventually came for my monthly payment, which at its lowest was $400 a month! That was more than my car note! I was hopeful I wouldn't have to pay this loan my entire life, but it was clear it was going to be my reality for the next decade or longer. I was so annoyed. Eighty-thousand dollars showed up on my credit report when the list of all the student loans was tallied. I felt bamboozled by the system. I wasn't making that much as it was.

It was at this moment, with a son no more than two years old, when I started thinking about life insurance and college savings. I was kicking into Momma Bear mode and wanted to make sure my cub was protected. I took pride in being a present parent, so my day-to-day focus shifted after he was born to being actively involved in his academic, social, and spiritual growth to ensure he was best set up with the exposure and resources he needed to build his rich life when he reached adulthood. I bought a whole life policy and started a MD 529 investment plan to start saving in a fund specifically for my son's college education. These were two of the best chess moves I made in my twenties when it came to investing. That 529 still helps us through those private college tuition payments every semester! Big wins happen when starting sooner than later. Don't worry, you can still win even if you're just starting today. The goal is to learn and grow your knowledge, so you understand market fluctuations and associated risk levels.

Street Truth: Invest for Your Future Now

It's tempting to believe that if you don't have thousands to invest, you might as well hold off from doing anything with your money. That's a Hood Life belief. You don't need a fortune to start, what you need, as I've said before, is discipline and consistency. Those who make it forward know it's not about having a lot to invest, it's about growing what you have.

Here's the reality: Time is your best friend when it comes to investing, but is often seen as limited and fast sailing when it comes to the joys of life. Time is certainly a more valuable asset than money, because you don't get it back. Memories of the joys life brings help us to value time even more. Remember to align your time with people, places, and things that push you closer to your rich life vision.

Biblical Wisdom: Diversify Your Efforts.

As duly noted in Ecclesiastes 11:2, which opens this chapter, is powerful because it encourages diversification, the concept of not putting all your eggs in one basket.

Real World Information – The Basics of Financial Investing

01 Start Small and Grow

Again, beginning with a small amount of money will add to your future more than no money will.

- Invest in fractional shares: Many investment apps allow you to buy parts of stocks with as little as $1.
- Try dollar-cost averaging (DCA): This is the strategy of investing a fixed amount of money regularly, no matter the market conditions. This helps to reduce the risk of market timing and smooths out the highs and lows.

    For example: Let's say you decide to invest $100 every month into a stock or exchange-traded fund (ETF), no matter what the price is.

Month 1:   The price is $10 per share
→ You buy 10 shares.

Month 2:   The price rises to $20 per share
→ You buy 5 shares.

Month 3:   The price drops to $5 per share
→ You buy 20 shares.

After three months, you've invested a total of $300 and purchased 35 shares.

If you had tried to "time the market" and invested all $300 in Month 2 when the price was $20, you'd only have 15 shares. By spreading out your investment, DCA allowed you to buy more shares when prices were low and fewer when prices were high, lowering your average cost per share over time.

- Use tax-advantaged accounts: 401(k)s, IRAs, and Roth IRAs are excellent ways to invest while getting tax benefits, especially if you have a long-term perspective with match programs with your employer.

    For example: Let's say your salary is $50,000 a year. If you decide to contribute 5% of your salary to your 401(k), that's $2,500 annually (or about $208 a month).

    If your employer offers a dollar-for-dollar match up to 5%, they will also contribute $2,500 into your account.

    That means instead of just saving $2,500 on your own, you now have $5,000 going into your retirement every year, without doing any extra work. Over time, with compound growth, that "free money" from your employer can add up to tens of thousands of dollars.

02 Index Funds and Exchange Traded Funds

Index funds and exchange-traded funds (ETFs) are one of the easiest ways to begin investing. This is because they offer:

- Low Fees: These funds track the performance of a stock market index. A stock market index is a way to measure the overall performance of a group of stocks. Think of it like a scoreboard; it shows how a particular section of the market is doing, such as large companies, tech companies, or the overall economy, like the S&P 500. Therefore, they generally have low fees and can be easily bought through most brokerage accounts.
- Diversification: They automatically diversify your investments by spreading your money across multiple companies or industries.

- Growth Potential: Historically, the S&P 500 has averaged about 7%–10% return per year, which can grow exponentially over time.

03 Know the Difference: Stocks vs. Bonds

- Stocks represent partial ownership in a company. They can grow fast, but they are considered a riskier investment vehicle.
- Bonds are loans to companies or governments, which pay interest over time. They are generally less risky than stocks, but they return a lower interest rate on your money.

04 Don't Let Fear Stop You

Market downturns are scary, especially for beginners. But here's the key:

- The market goes up and down, but over time, it trends upward. Don't panic sell when stocks dip. Investing for future Rise Rich goals is about long-term growth.
- Stay the course: If you invest in something solid like an index fund, and you contribute regularly, you will see growth over time.

"For the vision is yet for an appointed time, but at the end it will speak, and it will not lie. Though it tarries, wait for it" (Hab. 2:3).

05 Invest in What You Understand

If you're new to investing, don't rush into things you don't comprehend. It's better to start slow and learn about your options, rather than fall to pressure.

- Invest in what you know. If you understand the tech world, maybe start with tech stocks or funds. If you understand the real estate market, consider REITs (Real Estate Investment Trusts).
- Learn as you grow. It's okay to make mistakes but educate yourself along the way. Do not let one misstep derail you from the investment track.

Beginner's Guide to Investment Platforms

Here's the plan: Start small. Stay consistent. Let your money grow. Investing doesn't have to be complicated or reserved for the wealthy. Thanks to online platforms and apps, anyone can begin building wealth with just a few dollars and a little bit of discipline.

This section will walk you through some of the most common types of platforms where you can start your investing journey, such as retirement accounts, robo-advisors, and brokerage accounts. The goal isn't to overwhelm you with options, but to give you a clear starting point so you can choose the platform that best matches your goals and comfort level.

Remember, the earlier you begin, the more powerful time and compound growth will be in your favor. Don't worry if you can only start with small amounts, what matters most is building the habit of consistent investing and allowing your money to work for you.

01 Acorns

Best for: People who want to invest spare change automatically

- **How it works:** Rounds up your purchases to the nearest dollar and invests the difference in ETFs
- **Minimum to start:** $5
- **Pros:** Super easy, automatic, good for beginners
- **Cons:** Monthly fee ($3–$5), even for small accounts
- **Rise Tip:** Great "set it and forget it" app if you don't want to think too hard

02 Fidelity or Charles Schwab

Best for: Beginners looking to grow into long-term investors

- **How it works:** Full-service brokerage with $0 trading fees on stocks, ETFs, and index funds
- **Minimum to start:** $0 (you can invest small amounts in fractional shares)
- **Pros:** Reputable, low fees, huge selection of funds
- **Cons:** Online dashboard may feel overwhelming at first
- **Rise Tip:** Use their Roth IRA or brokerage account to build long-term wealth

03 Robinhood

Best for: Learning to trade stocks and ETFs quickly

- **How it works:** Commission-free trading app for stocks, ETFs, and crypto
- **Minimum to start:** $1
- **Pros:** Easy interface, instant trades
- **Cons:** No retirement accounts, encourages risky behavior if not careful

- **Rise Tip:** Only use this if you plan to educate yourself, don't treat it like a casino

04 Betterment or Wealthfront
Best for: Passive investors who want a "hands-off" approach

- **How it works:** Robo-advisors that manage your portfolio automatically based on your goals
- **Minimum to start:** $10
- **Pros:** Automated investing, tax-smart strategies
- **Cons:** Management fees (0.25%), no control over individual stocks
- **Rise Tip:** Great for people who want expert help without paying a human advisor

05 M1 Finance
Best for: Beginners who want automation + control

- **How it works:** Build custom "pies" of stocks or funds and automate your investing
- **Minimum to start:** $100
- **Pros:** Hybrid of DIY and robo-investing, no trading fees
- **Cons:** Not ideal for frequent traders or crypto fans
- **Rise Tip:** Choose pre-built expert pies if you're unsure where to start

06 Public
Best for: Social learners who want to invest with context

- **How it works:** Invest in stocks, ETFs, and crypto, plus see what others are investing in
- **Minimum to start:** $1

- **Pros:** Social feed helps you learn, fractional shares available
- **Cons:** Can encourage FOMO (fear of missing out) if you're not focused
- **Rise Tip:** Use it to learn, not copy. Stick to what aligns with your plan.

Investing Time in Networking and Relationships

Money and skills are powerful investments, but relationships are what multiply opportunities. Networking is more than just handing out business cards or adding contacts on LinkedIn; it's about intentionally building connections with people who can open doors, share knowledge, and walk with you on your journey. When you invest time in building relationships, you're planting seeds that may not grow immediately but can produce life-changing opportunities down the road. That could look like grabbing coffee with a mentor, showing up to industry events, joining professional groups, or simply checking in on people you respect. Networking expands your circle of influence, introduces you to opportunities you might never find on your own, and gives you access to wisdom and perspectives that can accelerate your growth. Strong relationships can lead to job offers, partnerships, collaborations, or lifelong friendships that enrich your personal and professional life.

Be mindful that networking also takes time and effort. Not every connection will lead to immediate results, and some relationships may turn out to be transactional rather than genuine. The key is to focus on building authentic connections, not just using people for gain. Understand that who you know can change what you grow. You could have all the talent in the world, but without the right people to recommend you, support you, or invest in you, your progress may be slower. Investing time into relationships isn't optional, it's part of building a rich life.

> ## If you hang around 5 millionaires, you're bound to be the 6th!

 ## *Rise Rich Exercise:*
Financial Investing Beginner's Checklist

The checklist below is designed to baby step you through starting your first investment. Be sure to confirm, check the box, then proceed down the list.

STEP 1: Get Clear on Your Goals

- ○ I know what I am investing toward (retirement, freedom, wealth, children's future, etc.).
- ○ I want to start seeing results in the short-term vs. long-term.
- ○ Even if it's small, I can afford to invest this amount ($ ....) each month (fill in the blank with a realist amount you can maintain).

STEP 2: Learn the Basics

- ○ I understand the difference between stocks, bonds, ETFs, and index funds.
- ○ I know why diversifying matters and have an idea of what I want to do.
- ○ I understand that investing is for the long-term, not quick flips/fast money.

STEP 3: Choose a Platform

○ I picked a beginner-friendly app or platform (Acorns, Fidelity, Betterment, etc.). Tip: Don't overthink it. The best platform is the one you'll actually use.

○ I created my account and linked my bank or debit card.

○ I set up two-factor authentication for account security.

STEP 4: Make Your First Move

○ I started with at least $5–$100, which I plan to grow as I comfortably can.

○ I chose an investment asset (index fund, ETF, or diversified portfolio).

○ I made my first deposit or trade.

STEP 5: Automate and Track

○ I set up automatic weekly/monthly transfers.

○ I committed to leaving the money invested. I will not make panic withdrawals.

○ I'll check progress once a month—not every day.

STEP 6: Keep Learning and Growing

○ I follow 1–2 trusted financial voices or podcasts.

○ I stay focused on my goals, not hype or social media trends.

○ I remind myself: Building wealth is a long game.

Journal Entry #10
Write & Reflect: Intentional Investments

01 What is one thing I can invest in today, no matter how small? (it can be in terms of time or money)

....

....

....

02 What asset or industry do I feel curious about or knowledgeable in?

....

....

....

03 What financial goal can I start working on to afford my first investment?

....

....

....

Fill in the blanks:

04 "I invest because

....

....

...."

05 "I'm building wealth so that I can

....

....

...."

Take One Step Closer to Your Rich Life

Remember, wealth is built over time. Millionaires don't wake up one day with bank accounts stuffed with money. Don't wait until you feel "ready" or until you think you have more money or time. Start now. Choose one small step that aligns with your rich life vision. For example:

- Financial Investment: Open a retirement account, set up an automatic transfer into an index fund, or put aside $25 this month into a high-yield savings account.
- Time Investment: Block out one hour this week to learn a new skill, reach out to someone who inspires you, or map out your personal financial goals.

These choices may seem small, but over time they compound into freedom, opportunity, and legacy. Every dollar invested and every hour directed with intention is a seed for the rich life you are building.

You don't need a financial advisor to dictate what you must do. You just need a decision and a little self-discipline. The more you invest in yourself, how you spend your time and your financial future, the more you'll build a quality rich life.

11   Understanding Income Taxes – A Foundation for Beginners

Taxes are one of those things everyone must deal with but very few people fully understand. Whether you're working a 9 to5, running a side hustle, or chasing your first, big, business dream, income taxes will touch your money. And here's the truth: ignoring taxes won't make them go away. The more you understand the basics, the more confident and in control you'll feel when tax season comes around. This chapter gives you the foundations you need to know, without all the complicated jargon, so you can manage your money with wisdom and intention.

My Story

I kept things simple when I first started working. As a rule of thumb, I always claimed two exemptions, myself and the head of household. Leaving my son for my husband to claim because even though we were married, we often filed separately to try and maximize our income tax return. That usually worked out well for me, but my husband always found a way to owe, until we learned how to leverage a business for additional tax exemptions. I typically ended up with a small refund at the end of the year. It felt like a safe formula that didn't require me to overthink the process.

Things shifted once I got married. Suddenly, we had to decide whether to file jointly or separately. Plus, our financial picture looked different from when I was single. Year after year, as our income increased, we found ourselves moving into higher tax brackets, which changed how much we owed. What once felt simple became more complex, and I realized that taxes weren't just about filing paperwork, they were about strategy.

Entrepreneurship added another layer, but in many ways, it worked to our advantage. Running a business gave us access to tax write-offs we had never considered before, from home office expenses to business-related travel and supplies. This helped lower our taxable income while teaching us the importance of record-keeping and intentional planning.

Over time, we began to understand how to calculate our tax obligations more clearly. Instead of guessing, we learned how to determine the right number of exemptions to claim so we weren't stuck with a large bill or missing out on money we could use throughout the year. What started as a trial-and-error approach turned into a growing awareness of how to use the tax system wisely, not fearfully.

 Street Truth: Understanding the Fundamentals Removes the Fear

In the Hood, tax season often feels like the government is just taking money we don't have. Many people look forward to tax refunds as "bonus money," but the truth is, it's simply your own money being returned because too much was taken from your paycheck during the year. The real play isn't to rely on a refund but to learn how to manage your taxes, so you keep more of your money throughout the year. That begins with understanding the basics.

Income tax is money you pay to the government based on what you earn, whether that's wages, salaries, tips, side hustle income, or even investment gains. These taxes are collected at the federal level, and in many states and localities as well, to fund the programs and services we use every day, from schools and healthcare to roads, security, and national defense.

Typically, taxes are automatically taken out of your paycheck in a process called withholding. This means you never actually see the full gross amount you earned, because your employer sends part of it directly to the government on your behalf. But if you earn money outside of traditional employment, whether through a side hustle, freelancing, or running a small business, you are responsible for setting aside your own tax payments. These are called self-employment taxes, and they cover both your income tax and your contributions to Social Security and Medicare.

Another important concept is tax brackets. The United States uses a progressive tax system, which means the more you earn, the higher the percentage you pay on that portion of your income. A common misconception is that moving into a higher tax bracket means your entire paycheck is taxed at that rate. In reality, only the income that falls within each bracket is taxed at that percentage, while the rest is taxed at lower rates. Be sure you understand the tax laws for your country, state, and county by researching the official tax authority's website.

You should also be familiar with common tax forms you're likely to encounter. Depending on your specific situation, you may be required to submit one or more of them with your tax return. In the United States (U.S.):

- The W-2 summarizes your yearly wages and taxes paid if you are an employee.
- The 1099 reports income earned from self-employment, freelance, or contract work.
- The 1040 is the main form individuals file with the IRS to determine whether they owe additional taxes or are due a refund.

When you are just starting out, tax season can feel like a test you didn't study for. The good news is that taxes don't have to be overwhelming. Whether you should prepare your own or hire a professional depends on your situation, your comfort level, and your long-term financial goals. Filing your own taxes can be empowering and cost-effective, especially when your financial life is simple. For many young adults, this means having one job with only a W-2 form, no property or dependents, and taking the standard deduction. With free online tools like IRS Free File or entry-level filing software, it's possible to complete a return in under an hour. Doing it yourself builds confidence and financial literacy while keeping more money in your pocket.

As your financial picture grows more complex, however, it may be worth hiring a tax preparer. Professional help can save you time, stress, and even money when you have freelance or side hustle income, own a business or LLC, invest in stocks or cryptocurrency, buy a home, move between states, or claim dependents and complicated credits. A qualified tax professional – whether a CPA, enrolled agent, or a company like H&R Block – can help you maximize deductions and provide peace of mind with audit support. While the cost of hiring a professional can range from a hundred dollars to several hundred, depending on complexity, their expertise often uncovers savings you might otherwise miss.

The decision comes down to trade-offs. Doing it yourself is cheaper and builds your financial knowledge, but it carries the risk of mistakes or missed deductions. Hiring a professional offers expert guidance and protection but comes with a higher price tag and the possibility of becoming dependent on others to handle your finances. The best approach is to start simple. If your taxes are straightforward, prepare them yourself at least once to gain the experience and understanding. That knowledge is powerful and reduces dependency. As your income streams expand and your financial life grows more layered, consider investing in professional help. Think of it the same way you might hire a trainer at the gym or a coach for your business – their expertise helps you maximize results and avoid costly mistakes.

Biblical Wisdom: Give What Is Owed – Even the Bible touches on the reality of taxes. In Mark 12:17, Jesus says, *"Give back to Caesar what is Caesar's, and to God what is God's."* Taxes are part of life, but stewardship is about learning how to handle all our resources wisely, including what belongs to the government.

Preparing for Tax Season

One of the best ways to reduce stress and avoid costly mistakes is to approach tax season with preparation rather than panic. Taxes don't have to feel overwhelming if you treat them as an annual checkpoint in your financial journey. The key is to stay organized all year, know your deadlines, and seize opportunities that put money back in your pocket.

The first step is organization. Create a tax folder – whether physical or digital – and make it a habit to add every important document as soon as you receive it. This includes W-2s, 1099s, bank statements, charitable donation receipts, and records of deductible expenses. If you have a side hustle, freelance work, or gig income, track both your earnings and related expenses. Keeping all your paperwork in one place saves time and makes sure nothing slips through the cracks.

Another essential part of preparation is knowing your deadlines. In the U.S., April 15 is the usual filing deadline, but self-employed individuals should also keep an eye on quarterly estimated tax due dates. Filing early has real benefits: you avoid last-minute stress, get your refund faster, and reduce the risk of identity theft. Planning ahead keeps you in control instead of scrambling under pressure.

It's also important to understand your personal situation. Review last year's return to identify which forms and documents you'll likely need again. Clarify your filing status, since being single, married, or head of household can change your available credits and deductions. Consider any life changes such as marriage, divorce, children, a new job, or relocation, as these can impact your tax obligations.

Being proactive can also help maximize your benefits. Contributing to retirement accounts like an IRA can lower your taxable income, and in some cases, you can make those contributions until the filing deadline. Don't forget to look into valuable credits like the Earned Income Tax Credit, education credits, or childcare credits. Review potential deductions, including charitable donations, student loan interest, and qualifying medical expenses. These are all opportunities to legally decrease what you owe or increase your refund.

Tax season is more than just paperwork – it's a chance to reflect on your financial habits, evaluate how money flows in and out of your life, and make smarter decisions for the future. By preparing early and approaching the process intentionally, you gain confidence, protect your resources, and ensure your money works for you instead of against you.

Rise Rich Exercise:
Your Rich Tax Strategy

To shift your perspective on taxes from something you "have to do" into a tool you intentionally manage to protect and grow your wealth, review the steps below, then set aside ample time to complete them.

STEP 1: Reflect on Last Year
Pull out your last tax return (or, if this is your first time, think about your current income streams). Write down:
- How much income you reported.
- How much tax you paid or how much of a refund you received.
- One area where you felt confused or unprepared.

STEP 2: Identify Your Growth Areas
Circle anything that surprised you or felt out of alignment with your Rich Life Vision. For example:
- Did your refund feel too small because you weren't prepared?
- Did you pay extra because you didn't track expenses?
- Did you miss deductions or credits you might qualify for?

STEP 3: Align with Your Rich Life

Write down how you want your taxes to serve your bigger goals. For example:

- If you're a side hustler, could tracking expenses more carefully lower your taxable income?
- If you're a young professional, could contributing to a retirement account help you save on taxes *and* build wealth?
- If you're building generational wealth, could tax planning with a pro protect your long-term strategy?

STEP 4: Set One Rich Tax Habit

Decide on one action to take this year that will make next tax season easier and more profitable. Examples:

- Create a monthly "tax folder" habit.
- Set aside a percentage of side hustle income for quarterly estimated taxes.
- Schedule a consultation with a tax advisor to learn about deductions and credits.

 ## Journal Entry #11
Write & Reflect: Be Prepared to Not Dread Tax Season

01 How do I usually feel about tax season – confident, confused, or stressed?

....

....

....

02 Have I ever thought about my refund as a tool for building wealth instead of "extra money"?

....

....

....

03 What would change if I treated taxes as something I manage instead of something I fear?

....

....

....

Take One Step Closer to Your Rich Life

Taxes don't have to be a mystery, a burden, or a reason to fear April every year. When you understand how income taxes work, you gain the power to plan ahead, keep more of your hard-earned money, and use it with intention. Remember, a refund is not a bonus, it's only your money being returned. The real win is learning how to manage your taxes ahead of tax season, so you control your income year-round instead of letting the system control you.

There is no reason to wait until tax season to get organized. Review your pay stub, pull out last year's return, and start paying attention to how much you earn, how much you pay, and where your money is going. The more informed you are, the less stressful taxes become, and the more confident you feel about using your money for your goals, not just government obligations.

This isn't about perfection; it's about stewardship. Each time you take responsibility for your numbers, you build a stronger financial foundation. Taxes are part of life, but when you master them instead of ignoring them, you step closer to freedom.

Bonus
Tax Season Checklist

Stay Organized

- ○ Create a tax folder (digital or physical)
- ○ Collect W-2s, 1099s, bank/interest statements, receipts, and deductible expenses
- ○ Track side hustle or freelance income and expenses

Know Your Deadlines

- ○ Mark April 15 (U.S.) or your country's filing date
- ○ Note quarterly estimated tax due dates if self-employed
- ○ File early to avoid stress and receive refunds faster

Understand Your Situation

- ○ Review last year's return as a guide
- ○ Confirm your filing status (single, married, head of household)
- ○ Account for life changes: marriage, divorce, children, moving, or new job

Maximize Benefits

○ Contribute to retirement accounts (IRA, 401(k), etc.)

○ Check eligibility for credits (EITC, education, childcare)

○ Review deductions (charitable giving, student loan interest, medical costs)

Decide How to File

○ Choose DIY software for simple returns

○ Hire a professional if you have multiple income streams, business income, or complex deductions

○ Prepare questions for your tax preparer about lowering next year's tax bill

12 The Power of Generosity and Giving Back

"It is more blessed to give than to receive"

– Acts 20:35

There is an important part of the Rise Rich vision that you need to see clearly: Wealth is not only about what you keep; it's about what you give.

We often think of wealth as what we can earn, save, or invest, but true wealth also flows through what we give. Money has power, but generosity multiplies that power far beyond what we could imagine. Giving back isn't just about writing checks. It's about creating impact, sowing into others, and shifting the culture of lack into one of abundance.

For many of us, the idea of giving may feel scary when we're still on our own journey toward financial freedom. But here's the truth: generosity is not about the size of your bank account, it's about the condition of your heart. Whether it's $5, an hour of your time, or a skill you share, giving back opens doors for blessings in ways money alone cannot.

Luke 6:38 says, "Give, and it will be given to you. A good measure, pressed down, shaken together and running over, will be poured into your lap."

When we give, we activate a principle of increase, for others and ourselves. Nobody builds lasting wealth by keeping everything to themselves. Communities grow when we pour into one another, and that's how legacies are created.

This chapter explores what it looks like to give with intention, whether through tithes, charitable donations, volunteering, or simply being generous in everyday life, as well as how giving back not only blesses others, but also fuels your rise to a rich life.

If you want to build a legacy that outlives you, giving must be part of your plan.

My Story

I was introduced to the importance of giving as a young girl. I loved visiting my Grandma Clytie on the weekends so we could have devotion on Saturday mornings and walk to church Sunday mornings. I looked forward to Grandma handing my brother and me her spare change so we had something to put in the tithing plate that came around when it was time for the church members to give. Tithing comes from the biblical principle of giving back one-tenth (10%) of your income to God. The word "tithe" literally means "tenth." The belief behind it is rooted in trust and obedience, recognizing that everything we have ultimately comes from God and returning a portion is an act of faith.

Tithing isn't just about money; it's about stewardship and surrender. In Malachi 3:10, God says, *"Bring the whole tithe into the storehouse, that there may be food in my house. Test me in this."* In this, He is declaring that obedience in giving opens the door to blessing. Many Christians believe tithing positions us for increase because it honors God first, invites provision, and keeps us from holding too tightly to what we have. In practical terms, tithing teaches discipline and generosity. It's not about giving out of guilt, but about giving out of gratitude and belief that God can do more with the 90% we keep than we could ever do with 100% on our own.

I joined my church, First Baptist Church of Glenarden, about ten years prior to the time of this writing, and me and my husband set our tithes on auto-payment then. This was after I had finished two discipleship programs that ultimately deepened my understanding of what it meant to tithe. It's now part of our way of life, and we are bound to it, as we believe we are under a covering from which blessings flow. Looking back, I realize when Grandma Clytie was sliding us change to put in the offering plate, she was planting seeds that taught us the importance of faithfulness. From first to last, I learned the power in giving, serving, and obedience.

Tithing is more than giving money to a church. It's a principle of faith and stewardship that opens the door for God to multiply what you have. I believe understanding the Lord's authority over our lives and the beneficial impact over our spiritual life that comes from being aligned with God's Word can truly add years to our lives and exponential amounts of dollars to our bank account balances.

The Bible promises in Malachi 3:10 that when we bring the tithe, God will *"throw open the floodgates of heaven"* with blessings. Yet, be aware that blessings don't always show up in monetary form. It often comes as unexpected provision, new opportunities, financial wisdom, and supernatural favor that stretches what you already have. Over time, this consistent discipline of giving can lead to exponential financial growth, not because of luck, but because God honors obedience.

Tithing can also add time to your life. Stress over money is one of the biggest causes of burnout, health issues, and broken relationships. When you tithe, you not only invite God's provision but also His peace. This changes your perspective from fear to trust, if you allow it, and that release of stress can literally give you more years and a better quality of life. Proverbs 3:9–10 reminds us, *"Honor the Lord with your wealth, with the first fruits of all your crops; then your barns will be filled to overflowing."*

In short, as a Christian I believe tithing doesn't subtract 10%, it multiplies the remaining 90%. It adds dollars to your balance through God's provision and wisdom, and it adds life to your years by removing the weight of financial fear and replacing it with peace, purpose, and overflow.

 Street Truth: Money doesn't change you, it reveals you

Some people think, *"I'll give when I make more."* But that mindset is backwards. If you won't give when you have a little, you won't give when you have a lot.

Whether you're giving time, money, or wisdom, generosity creates room for more. It shifts your focus from lack to abundance. Like I wrote before, that's moving from Hood Rich thinking to Rise Rich thinking.

Why Giving Matters

01 It Keeps You Humble and Grateful
- Giving can remind you of your roots, your lineage, or where you grew up.
- It helps you see others who have less and need what you already have.

02 It Helps You Stay Purpose-Driven

- You're not just chasing a number. You're building something that serves others.
- It puts your money in service of your Rise Rich vision of your faith, values, and legacy, making your rise of greater impact to your family and future generations.

03 It Builds Community

- Whether it's your church, your neighborhood, or a nonprofit, your money can move mountains for someone else.

Practical Ways to Give on Any Budget

"I'm still broke, should I still give?" This is a natural and common question. But generosity is not about how much you have. It's about your posture.

Jesus praised the poor widow who gave two small coins—not because of the amount, but because she gave from the heart. (Luke 21:1–4)

It's perfectly okay to start small. Be intentional about giving in one of the following ways. In fact, pick one or two as a challenge to put into action this week/month.

- Hold the door for a person with a lot of packages or a parent with a stroller.
- Give $1 to someone in need.
- Spend 10 minutes helping a neighbor.
- Make a phone call to encourage someone
- Sponsor a child or family

- Make a pledge to a local organization
- Offer free tutoring
- Volunteer to help at a charity event or fundraiser

The size of the effort or dollar amount doesn't matter.
The habit does.

Biblical Wisdom: Giving Is a Core Wealth Principle

Proverbs 11:25 says, *"A generous person will prosper; whoever refreshes others will be refreshed."*

The Bible doesn't just suggest giving, Jesus calls us to it. Giving:

- breaks the grip of greed
- protects your heart from pride
- aligns your purpose with something bigger than yourself

Giving to Bless Others

Jesus doesn't state money is the only thing a person is allowed to tithe or share with others. Beyond money, you can give:

- Time – volunteering, mentoring, helping a friend in need
- Skills – teaching others what you've learned, sharing advice when asked
- Opportunities – recommending someone for a job or sharing a connection
- Kindness – listening, random acts of kindness, sharing a smile

There are about 37 distinct miracles attributed to Jesus, including healing the sick, feeding thousands, calming storms, and raising the dead. You won't ever be able to match Jesus' giving energy, but you can definitely be intentional about giving and being a blessing to others. You can be the blessing you used to pray for. Enjoy spreading the wealth!

Rise Rich Exercise: Giving Goals Tracker

Generosity works best when it's intentional. Just like you track your income, savings, and debt payoff, it's powerful to track your giving. A giving goals tracker helps you plan ahead, stay consistent, and actually see the impact of your generosity over time. Whether you tithe faithfully, support charities, or simply look for ways to bless others, this exercise will help you align your giving with your financial vision.

Remember, giving isn't about the dollar amount, it's about the heart and the habit. By writing it down and reviewing your progress, you'll not only stay on track, but also begin to notice how giving shapes your life, your peace, and your purpose.

Follow these next few steps to:

- Stay intentional with generosity.
- Create a habit that aligns with your values.
- Celebrate impact, not just income.
- Build a legacy of service and stewardship.

STEP 1: Define Your Giving Vision

- Why do I want to give?

  ....

  ....

  ....

- What causes or groups of people matter most to me?

  ....

  ....

  ....

- How do I want to make a difference this year?

  ....

  ....

  ....

STEP 2: Select and Set Your Giving Goals

- Tithes/Giving to Church
- Support Local Organization that aligns with your values
- Random Acts of Kindness
- Volunteer Time
- Sponsor or Scholarship

STEP 3: Track Monthly Giving (Time + Money)

MONTH	AMOUNT GIVEN	TIME VOLUNTEERED	WHO / WHERE DID I GIVE?	HOW DID IT FEEL?
January				
February				
March				
April				
May				
June				
July				
August				
September				
October				
November				
December				

STEP 4: Monthly Giving Reflection

- What did I learn from giving this month? What do I want more or less of?

....

....

....

- What stories or moments impacted me the most? What feelings or emotions made me feel good?

....

....

....

- How can I give more intentionally next month?

....

....

....

"Each of you should give what you have decided in your heart to give" (2 Cor. 9:7).

Journal Entry #12
Write & Reflect: Giving Isn't an Option

01 When did someone give me something that changed my life? What was it? How might I use that as inspiration to help the next person?

....

....

....

02 What can I give today, even if it's small?

....

....

....

03 How does giving fit into the legacy I want to leave?

....

....

....

Take One Step Closer to Your Rich Life

At the end of the day, giving is not just about money, it's about mindset, stewardship, and legacy.

> Wealth is empty if it only flows to you
> and never through you.

When you give, you declare that money is a tool, not your master. You sow seeds that can outlast you, blessing others while also opening doors for your own increase.

> The world may tell you to hold on tight,
> but God's Word shows us all that generosity
> unlocks abundance.

Luke 6:38 reminds us, "Give, and it will be given to you… pressed down, shaken together, and running over." Your rich life isn't only measured by what you've built, it's measured by the impact you leave. Whether it's through tithing, donations, service, or simply showing up for others, giving multiplies your influence and secures your legacy. The more you release, the more room you create for God to fill your hands again.

So, take one step closer to your rich life by choosing generosity. Decide today not just to build wealth, but to share it in ways that outlive you. Because the greatest return on investment is not solely in your bank account, it's in the lives you touch.

13 Your Legacy Starts with You

"A good person leaves an inheritance for their children's children" (Prov, 13:22).

You've made it this far. That alone makes you different. Most people only *wish* for change. You've taken actual steps toward it. Even if that's the baby step of reading this book and putting some of its ideas into action.

Now, it is time to focus on the last steps of bringing the Rise Rich mindset home. You're not just building wealth; you're building a legacy. In this chapter we'll explore what it really means to build a legacy: passing down wisdom, creating generational wealth, and setting up systems that break cycles instead of repeating them. That's because your rich life isn't complete until it outlasts you.

To those with a Rise Rich mindset, legacy isn't just what you leave behind after you're gone. It's what you're living out now, every day.

 Street Truth: Your legacy doesn't start at the will reading. It starts with today's decisions.

My Story

When I started looking beyond the day-to-day demands of budgeting and taxes, I asked myself a bigger question: *How can I make sure my family is financially secure for generations to come?* That question led me to what's known as the Rockefeller Method. Named after John D. Rockefeller, this approach is centered on using life insurance, trusts, and intentional planning to create wealth that not only lasts a lifetime but also provides guidance, protection, and opportunity for the generations that follow.

I chose this method because I realized wealth isn't just about having money – it's about building a system that preserves and multiplies resources while instilling values. Too many families work hard only to see their progress lost in the next generation due to lack of structure or financial literacy. By adopting the Rockefeller Method, I committed to protecting my family from that cycle. I wanted my children and their children to have access to opportunities, education, and a safety net – while also being held accountable to steward that wealth wisely.

Before pursuing this path, there are **important steps to consider:**

01 **Educate Yourself –** Understand how whole life insurance and trusts actually work, and be clear about long-term commitments.

02 **Assess Your Goals –** What do you want your money to do beyond your lifetime? Is it college funding, family businesses, philanthropy, or legacy giving?

03 **Build a Team** – Work with trusted advisors such as financial planners, estate attorneys, and tax professionals who understand generational wealth strategies.

04 **Start Small, Then Scale** – You don't need Rockefeller money to begin. Start with a policy or trust that fits your budget and expand as your wealth grows.

05 **Teach the Next Generation** – Wealth without wisdom can become a burden. Pair financial resources with clear values and guidance.

The **benefits of establishing this system** are powerful. It ensures that your family has access to resources while keeping those resources protected from unnecessary taxes, lawsuits, and reckless spending. It creates an inheritance of both financial capital and family values. Most importantly, it shifts the mindset from *short-term survival* to *long-term stewardship*. Instead of wealth disappearing within one or two generations, it becomes a wellspring that funds education, business ventures, and even charitable missions – all while keeping the family's vision intact.

Choosing the Rockefeller Method was my way of saying: *Debt ends with me, but wealth begins here.* It was a decision not just for my children, but for their children too. And that's what building a rich life is all about – not just living well today, but creating a structure so that those who come after us have the wisdom and resources to rise even higher.

You can't take money with you when you're gone, but you can leave behind the impact of how you used it. Too many people spend their lives hustling just to get by, never realizing that every dollar, every decision, and every sacrifice has the power to outlive them. Legacy isn't just about leaving cash; it's about leaving change.

When you live with intention, you begin to see the wealth you're building today is not only for your bills, your vacations, or even your retirement. It's also for your children, your family, and your community. Legacy is about planting seeds for trees you may never sit under but knowing someone else will find their shade. It's the difference between money that dies when you do and wealth that continues to work long after you're gone.

Biblical Wisdom: Legacy Is Intentional

Deuteronomy 6:6–7 says, *"These commandments...are to be on your hearts. Impress them on your children."* That's the foundation of generational living.

You don't need to have millions to leave a legacy. You need vision, consistency, and God-led principles. When you walk in faith and financial wisdom, you are not continuing the curse, you're confronting it. You are doing spiritual and financial warfare, and that's not light work. But here's the good news: You are equipped for it. You don't just heal for you; you heal for those who will come after you.

Generational Curses

Generational curses are negative patterns, behaviors, or struggles that seem to pass down through families from one generation to the next. These can show up in many forms, such as poverty, debt cycles, broken relationships, addictions, poor health choices, or even destructive mindsets about money and success.

From a biblical perspective, generational curses are often described as the consequences of sin or disobedience that continue through a family line until they are broken through faith and obedience to God (see Exodus 20:5–6). The good news is that through Christ, we have the power to break those cycles and create new legacies for our children and grandchildren.

From a practical perspective, generational curses can look like inherited habits. If your parents never learned how to manage money, chances are you didn't either. If debt, overspending, or financial stress were "normal" in your household, it might feel natural to repeat those same behaviors unless you make a conscious choice to change.

You may have inherited the fight, but you don't have to pass it on. Generational curses and strongholds are real.

However, just because something was normal doesn't mean it was right. Generational curses are breakable. Generational curses are cycles of struggle that keep repeating until someone decides they end here. Debt ends with me. Lack ends with me. Fear around money ends with me. When you choose to break these strongholds, you're not just changing your story, you're rewriting your family's future.

Signs You're Breaking the Chain

Breaking the chains that have bound your family starts with recognizing that you don't have to repeat the past. Spiritually, it's about surrendering the old patterns to God and declaring that those cycles of lack, debt, or fear end with you. Prayer, faith, and obedience are the weapons that tear down those strongholds. It looks like declaring, *"I am no longer bound by what held my family back. In Christ, I am free to build something new."*

On a practical level, breaking the chains looks like:

- Learning what your parents didn't know – budgeting, saving, and investing.
- Saying "no" to debt, even when the world says, "swipe now, pay later."
- Choosing to tithe or give when you were taught to hold on tight.
- Opening a savings account for your child when no one did it for you.
- Writing down goals and planning instead of just "getting by."

Breaking generational curses is like cutting the padlock off what has been keeping your family tied to purposefully unfruitful behaviors. Maybe your parents and grandparents were weighed down by debt, living check to check, or never got a chance to own property. When you choose to learn, to save, to invest, to budget with intention, you're snapping those locks, one by one, and opening doors that your family never had the keys to. The work happens not in one big, dramatic event; it's consistent small choices that add up to a completely different story than the one you inherited.

- You say "no" to spending to impress and "yes" to saving for freedom.
- You talk openly about money, debt, and healing—even when it's uncomfortable.
- You stop hiding from your past and start building on truth.
- You parent differently, plan differently, think differently.

Rise Rich Exercise:
Generational Freedom Action Plan

Generational curses lose their power when you identify them and make a conscious choice to replace them with new, life-giving patterns. This exercise will help you name the chains you've seen in your family and map out the new legacy you want to create.

STEP 1: Identify Strongholds

Before you break generational chains, you have to name them.

WHAT I INHERITED	WHAT I CHOOSE TO BUILD INSTEAD
Example: Fear of money	Confidence through knowledge and budgeting
Example: Living paycheck to paycheck	Living on purpose with margins
Example: Silence around finances	Honest conversations about money and growth

STEP 2: Break the Cycle Intentionally

Breaking curses require actions of discipline and faith and making decisions that feel uncomfortable at first but freeing later.

Answer these questions:

- What's one new money habit I'm starting this month?
- What's one lie about money I'm letting go of?
- Who in my life needs to see me model something different?

STEP 3: Pass on New Patterns

Fill in the blanks below to define your new legacy:

My family will no longer

....

....

We will now

....

....

I will teach my children/family/community to

....

....

In five years, our story will look like

....

....

STEP 4: Write Your Family Legacy Code

This is a short declaration of the principles your family will live and grow by. It is a vision statement to guide your path, serving as a set of guardrails.

My family's example:

We are builders, not borrowers. We give freely, live wisely, and lead with integrity.
We honor God with our money and our mission. We break cycles. We walk in freedom.

Now you write yours:

....

....

....

....

....

....

....

....

....

....

....

 **Journal Entry #13**
Write & Reflect: **Changing Legacy Tides**

01 What financial chain am I most determined to break?

....

....

....

02 What kind of legacy do I want to leave – spiritually, financially, relationally?

....

....

....

03 What is one habit I can start today that reflects my future legacy?

....

....

....

04 Who can I mentor, share with, or uplift with what I've learned?

....

....

....

Take One Step Closer to Your Rich Life

You are the blueprint. The legacy for those after you will be built on the foundations you are building. Remember, you're not just saving money, you're saving generations.

You might have come from a family that didn't talk about money.

You might be the first one to imagine and strive for something different.

That's not something costing you. That's not a disadvantage.

That's your assignment.

You're breaking strongholds, walking in freedom, and leaving a trail for others to follow.

And, you are doing so by example.

So, go build wisely. Go give freely. Go live boldly.
Because legacy isn't left by the loudest. It's left by the most consistent.

> "You were born looking like your parents.
> You die looking like your decisions."

— Crawford Loritts, attributed

Your Rise Rich Declaration: I Am the One

I am the one.

The one who stops the cycle.

The one who rewrites the story.

The one who builds what was never built for me.

Not by pride. By purpose.

Not by power. By the grace of God.

I don't pass on pain—I pass on freedom.

The curse stops with me. The blessing starts with me.

I am the one.

Daily Affirmations for the Journey Ahead

Speak these aloud. Declare them often. Let them reshape your mindset.

01 I am not behind — I am starting exactly where I need to.
I release shame and comparison. My journey is mine, and I honor it.

02 I am breaking cycles and building systems.
What my family didn't know, I'm learning. What they didn't build, I will.

03 I have everything I need to begin.
Wisdom. Discipline. Faith. God will multiply what I steward.

04 I do not chase money — I command it with purpose.
My money has a mission. I am not a slave to it. It serves my goals, not my fears.

05 I spend intentionally, save consistently, and give generously.
My budget is not a restriction, it's a declaration of my freedom.

06 I enjoy life while I build wealth.
Fun and finances can coexist. I don't wait until "someday" to live.

07 I am not just creating change, I am the change.
I'm setting a new standard for those watching me, near and far.

08 I sow in faith and expect a harvest.
Whether through giving, saving, or serving, nothing is wasted.

09 I lead my money — I don't let it lead me.
I walk in wisdom, and I consult God before culture.

10 I am the blueprint. The blessing begins with me.
Wealth starts here. Legacy lives on from here.

Say it. Live it. Become it.

A Concluding Message from the Author

To the one who's ready for change...

You may not know me personally, but if you made it to this page, I feel like I know something about you.

You've felt the weight of starting from scratch.

You've watched others build while you were trying to survive.

You've prayed for more, not just for yourself, but for future generations. And now, you're ready to do something about it.

I wrote this book because I've been where you are.

I grew up in a low-income environment, surrounded by lack and survival mentality.

No trust funds. No money talks. No blueprint.

But I knew deep down: *There has to be another way.*

And God showed me: there is.

I started small. I made mistakes.

I relearned everything I thought I knew about money, faith, and freedom.

And now, I'm still growing, still building.

But I'm doing it on purpose—and you can too.

This book isn't just about money. It's about mindset, mission, and movement.

It's about breaking generational strongholds with God at the center.

It's about letting go of shame, fear, and false definitions of success.

It's about walking boldly into the life you were born to live, even if no one before you did.

If no one ever told you this, let me say it clearly:

- You are not too late.
- You are not too broken.
- You are not too behind.

You are exactly who God can use to break the curse and build the legacy.

Every budgeting decision, every act of generosity, every financial boundary you set, it matters.

You're building something your future self, your children, and even your community will thank you for.

Wealth starts here. With you. With faith. With action.

I'm rooting for you!

With Rich Purpose,
LaChelle

Scan the QR code below to download your Rise Rich AI-Powered Personal Finance Coach and continue your journey!

www.ingramcontent.com/pod-product-compliance
Lightning Source LLC
Chambersburg PA
CBHW021109130626

46554CB00002B/599